FAMILY HISTORY
ON THE

2015/16

Colin Waters

COUNT........
NEWBURY BERKSHIRE

First published 2007
Text © Colin Waters 2007

Second edition 2009
Third edition 2011
Fourth edition 2013

Fifth edition 2015

A CIP record for this book is available from the British Library.

COUNTRYSIDE BOOKS
3 Catherine Road
Newbury, Berkshire

To view our complete range of books, please visit us at
www.countrysidebooks.co.uk

ISBN 978 1 84674 325 2

Produced through The Letterworks Ltd., Reading
Typeset by KT Designs, St Helens
Printed by Berforts Information Press, Oxford

CONTENTS

family history on the net

Introduction 5

National Archives 6

Family History Courses & Tutorials 6

Comprehensive Genealogy Sites & Search Engines 7

ALPHABETICAL SUBJECT GUIDE

Adoption 13

Archives, Libraries, Collections & Resources (the UK & Ireland) 13

Archives, Libraries, Collections & Resources (Overseas) 18

Bibles, Family 36

Births, Baptisms, Marriages, Divorces & Deaths 36

Cartularies, Charters & Historic Public Records 42

Census Returns 43

Charities, Institutions & the Poor 45

Chronology 50

Clans 51

Coats of Arms, Heraldry, Emblems & Flags 52

Copyright 53

Directories 53

DNA/Genetic Genealogy 53

Domesday Book 54

Education 54

Election Records 55

Emigration & Immigration 56

Family History Societies & Fairs 57

Fire Insurance 58

Freemen, Guilds & Livery Companies 59

Genealogical Research Services 60

Genealogy Chat Rooms, Forums, Look-ups, Message Boards
    & Mailing Lists 60

Genealogy Magazines 61
Hospitals & Asylums 61
Land & Property 63
Law & Order including Punishments, Criminals, Reform Schools, Prisons 65
Local History Societies & Groups 71
Manorial Records 71
Maps & Gazetteers 72
Medieval Genealogy 74
Newspaper & Magazine Resources 75
Nobility & Aristocracy 76
Occupations 76
Orders & Friendly Societies 102
Parliamentary & Political Records 106
Passports 108
Photography 109
Place-Names 110
Plaques, Inscriptions, Datestones, Statues & Sculptures 112
Reference Information 114
Religion 117
Shipping including Passenger & Crew Lists 126
Social Network Genealogy Sites 130
Sports and Sportsmen 130
Strays 131
Supplies & Services 131
Surnames 132
Taxation 134
Villages 136
Wartime & Military Resources 138
Wills, Administration, Probate & Death Duties 158

Introduction

Searching the Internet is by far the easiest and quickest way to find much of the information needed to compile a family history.

However, even regular users of the Internet can find it difficult to know where to start or which websites will be most useful to them on a particular subject. This book is designed to help solve these problems and to be easy to use, whether you are a complete beginner in family history research or an accomplished genealogist. In order to make using the book as easy as possible, these websites are grouped around particular subjects, in alphabetical order, and many will take you straight to the topic you are interested in. For example, if you are seeking genealogical information for any specific English county you need only look under 'England' in the *Archives, Libraries, Collections & Resources (the UK & Ireland)* section to find a website address that will lead to a full list of counties from which you can make your choice. This saves you from having to trawl through long lists of separate printed entries and also reduces the tedious task of continually typing lengthy website addresses. To aid selection, all entries are followed by a brief summary of their content, though as some sites are diverse in nature it will often be necessary to access a website in order to get a full picture of the exact format and type of information available. Care has been taken only to include sites that are of genuine use to the family historian. Those that are difficult to use or continually bombard the Internet user with advertisement 'pop-ups', or even worse lock the user onto their website making it difficult to leave, have been omitted.

With literally billions of websites available, it is inevitable that not every site can be listed in a book such as this and each category can only carry a selective sample of the multitude available. Also, because of the ever changing nature of the Internet, it is not impossible that some of those listed will change or close during the lifetime of this book. Nevertheless, because the same information is available from a number of sources, simply searching for a similar site under the same heading should solve this problem. Alternatively, appropriate sites can be reached by using one of the links in the first section of the book: *Comprehensive Genealogy Sites & Search Engines*.

With this book as your companion, you can be sure to make the best use of your 'surfing' experience.

NOTE TO THE 2015/2016 EDITION

This new edition contains a number of additional subject headings, including a selection of old newsreel sites under the 'Archives, Libraries, Collections & Resources' section. Readers will also find lots of new entries for countries and regions previously omitted. As in previous editions, every single entry has been scrupulously checked for accuracy.

Pages that are no longer active or correct have been deleted or amended and new entries have been added where appropriate. An attempt has also been made to streamline searches by omitting the entries for sub-pages that can be easily accessed using links on the main web page of any organisation already listed under any particular heading.

NATIONAL ARCHIVES

Records concerning virtually every category found in this book will be found at The National Archives. In order to avoid constantly repeating the website addresses unnecessarily, the main web pages for repositories in Britain, Ireland and overseas countries that have strong historic links to Britain, have been placed here at the beginning of the book for easy reference.

www.nationalarchives.gov.uk (Main website)
www.englishheritagearchives.org.uk/ (English Heritage Archives)
trove.nla.gov.au (Trove – Australia's National Library Archives)
www.nationalarchives.ie (National Archives of Irish Republic)
www.nas.gov.uk (National Archives of Scotland)
www.archiveswales.org.uk (Archives Wales)
www.llgc.org.uk (National Library of Wales)
www.proni.gov.uk (Northern Ireland Public Record Office)
www.naa.gov.au/ (National Archives of Australia)
archives.govt.nz/ (National Archives New Zealand)
www.national.archives.gov.za/ (South Africa National Archives)
www.collectionscanada.gc.ca/ (National Library and Archives of Canada)
nationalarchives.nic.in/ (National Archives of India)
www.archives.gov/ (U.S. National Archives)

FAMILY HISTORY COURSES & TUTORIALS

If you are new to researching your family tree, you should start here!

www.pharostutors.com (About free & paid online courses)
www.ihgs.ac.uk (Website of the Institute of Heraldic and Genealogical Studies, with details of courses)
www.learnwebskills.com/ (A beginner's guide to genealogy on the net)
www.bbc.co.uk/familyhistory/ (BBC guide to researching your family history)

COMPREHENSIVE GENEALOGY SITES & SEARCH ENGINES

Rather than type in long internet addresses, it is sometimes easier to go to a particular website's homepage and to click on the resource required. Below, in alphabetical order, are listed some of the more well-known sites dealing with the whole spectrum of genealogy. These can be used as an alternative means of access to many of the individual pages listed later in this book. More specialised listings will be found in the alphabetical subject guide. The sites listed in this section vary in design and purpose but on the whole provide a wide range of resources for the family historian, ranging from online documents and lists of names and addresses to facilities for searching for names, dates, events or places. Many also provide research tips, as well as links to other useful sites and records covering similar subjects. On the whole they are free to use, though you may have to register to get a password so as to access information. Others are partially free or only accessible by subscription. It is always worth checking whether the records you require are available free elsewhere on the Internet before subscribing to pay-to-use sites.

A2A
www.a2a.org.uk (Database containing catalogues describing over 10 million records held locally in England and Wales dating from the 8th century to the present day)

ABIKA
www.abika.com/Reports/verifyemail.htm (US-based site allowing the tracing of people past and present using various resources)

ABILITY
www.ability.org.uk/genealogy_searchable_databases.html (Links to specific genealogy search engines and databases)

ANCESTOR HUNT
www.ancestorhunt.com/ (Hundreds of Internet searches and links with a U.S. bias)

ANCESTRY
www.ancestry.co.uk/search/ (Search for your forebears by name, date or region)

ARCHIVES HUB
www.archiveshub.ac.uk/ (Search university and college archives)

AWESOME GENEALOGY

www.**awesomegenealogy.com/** (Heavily biased to American research)

BRITISH HISTORY ONLINE

www.**british-history.ac.uk/search.asp** (Useful for historic surnames or related places and occupations, as well as deeds, official records and documents of all kinds)

BRITISH ISLES GENEALOGY

www.**bigenealogy.com/** (Specifically caters for British, Irish and Channel Islands genealogy)

BRITISH ROOTS

www.**britishroots.plus.com** (Comprehensive British genealogy resources)

CORAWEB

www.**coraweb.com.au/index.htm** (An Australian site with some very useful UK links)

CYNDI'S LIST

www.**cyndislist.com/** (Considered to be one of the best free family history sites on the Internet. Though US-biased, Cyndi's List covers every subject imaginable concerning world-wide genealogy)

DMOZ

www.**dmoz.org/Society/Genealogy/** (Search for any name, address, date, phrase, etc. on the web)

FAMILY RELATIVES

www.**familyrelatives.com** (Links to a variety of family history resources on the web)

FAMILY SEARCH

www.**familysearch.org** (Search what is claimed to be the largest collection of free genealogy records in the world, provided by the LDS (Mormon) Church, including the IGI and 1881 census)

FAMILY TREE SEARCHER

www.**familytreesearcher.com/** (Searches multiple sites and gives tips on research)

Comprehensive Genealogy Sites & Search Engines

FIND MY PAST
www.findmypast.co.uk/ (Lots of resources – pay to view individual records or subscribe to view all)

FLICKR
www.flickr.com/ (Photo based website containing much historical material)

FREE-UK-GEN
freeukgen.rootsweb.com/ (A continuously expanding free resource for birth, marriage and death, census and other records)

GENEALOGIST, THE
www.thegenealogist.co.uk/ (Constantly growing pay-to-view site with many exclusive databases)

GENEALOGY UK
www.genealogy-of-uk.com/ (Comprehensive guide to searches, links & other resources)

GENEALOGY LINKS UK
www.genealogy-links.co.uk/ (UK genealogy links including those to specific counties)

GENEALOGY LINKS.NET
www.genealogylinks.net/ (Thousands of links to worldwide genealogy resources)

GENEALOGY TODAY
www.genealogytoday.com/ (Selection of both free and fee-based UK genealogy resources and searches)

GENES REUNITED
www.genesreunited.co.uk/ (Commercial site with many resources: search births, marriages and deaths and censuses using 300 million official records, plus contact facilities)

GENGATEWAY
www.gengateway.com/ (Gateways, links and guides to a vast array of genealogical information)

GENUKI SEARCH
www.genuki.org.uk/ (One of the most useful searches for genealogy records and databases on virtually any topic)

GENWEB
www.iukgenweb.org/ (British Isles genealogy with links to Genweb sites in other countries)

GIC (GLOBAL INFORMATION CENTRE)
www.gic.co.uk/roots.htm (Miscellaneous family history website links)

GOOGLE GENEALOGY
www.genealogy-search-help.com/ (A special search site for genealogists using Google, one of the most widely used search engines on the net)

GOOGLE TRANSLATE
translate.google.com/ Translate any foreign web page, phrase or word into English (Google Chrome offers this facility automatically)

INTERNATIONAL GENEALOGICAL INDEX
www.familysearch.org/Eng/Search/frameset_search.asp (Search the vast genealogical records held by the Mormon Church)

INTERNATIONAL GENEALOGICAL INDEX BATCH NUMBERS
tinyurl.com/3hvoj2 (Search the batch number records for any family history event in the UK and USA)

IRELAND GENEALOGY PROJECTS
irelandgenealogyprojects.rootsweb.com/ (Gateway linked to Irish genealogy)

MILITARY GENEALOGY
www.nmarchive.com/ (The Naval & Military archive for military historians and family genealogists)

MOCAVO
www.mocavo.com/ (Newly introduced genealogy search engine claiming to automate family research)

Comprehensive Genealogy Sites & Search Engines

MUNDIA
www.mundia.com/gb/ (A new family history site from Ancestry.com)

MYTREES.COM
www.mytrees.com/ (Can search using family relationships if you don't know the name of an ancestor)

OGRE
www.cefnpennar.com/index.htm (Name search with links to other useful family history resources)

ONE GREAT FAMILY
www.onegreatfamily.com/Home.aspx (General family history resources including photos, biographies and browsing by alphabet; free search but fees payable for other resources)

ORIGINS NET
www.origins.net/ (British and Irish genealogy resources with photos – membership required)

ROOTSWEB
www.rootsweb.com/ (Many facts and resources including records and actual family trees; has a strong US bias but also caters for British genealogists)
worldconnect.rootsweb.com/ (A Rootsweb project to connect family historians using Gedcom files – search what's available here)
resources.rootsweb.com/cgi-bin/metasearch (Searches using multiple search engines)

SCOTLANDS FAMILY
www.scotlandsfamily.com/links.htm (Also covers other British and overseas links and resources)

SCOTLANDS PEOPLE
http://www.scotlandspeople.gov.uk/ (Millions of wills, BMD and other Scottish records)

SILVER SURFERS
www.silversurfers.net/findit-people.html (Designed for the older user but provides everyone with a variety of resources and links to assist in finding people living or dead)

SOCIETY OF GENEALOGISTS

www.sog.org.uk/library/libindex.shtml (Genealogy resources from the respected Society of Genealogists)

SURNAMES SUPERSEARCH

surnamesupersearch.com/ (Multiple genealogy searches)

THE GENEALOGIST

www.thegenealogist.co.uk (Search for a wide variety of important records – Subscription site)

UK GENEALOGY ARCHIVES

uk-genealogy.org.uk (A wide variety of databases and links biased to UK research)

WORLD VITAL RECORDS

www.worldvitalrecords.com (Wide variety of unusual databases – Membership required)

YAHOO GENEALOGY

dir.yahoo.com/Arts/Humanities/History/Genealogy/ (Specialist genealogy search page on one of the oldest and most well used search engines on the net)

ALPHABETICAL SUBJECT GUIDE

ADOPTION

Official adoption only began in Britain on 1 January 1927. Before that time illegitimate, orphaned or otherwise homeless children were given up to childless families or were brought up by grandparents as the pretended sibling or cousin of their own actual parent. As a result, tracing these family connections can often prove a difficult task.

www.genealogy-guide.org.uk/adoption.html (General guide to all genealogy related adoption records)

www.gro-scotland.gov.uk/regscot/adoption.html (Official Scottish government site for all matters regarding adoption)

www.nas.gov.uk/guides/adoptions.asp (Adoption records in the Scottish National Archives)

www.adoptionsearchreunion.org.uk/default.htm (Adoption Search Reunion website)

www.ukbirth-adoptionregister.com/resources.php (UK adoption register – How to obtain your own or your child's adoption records in the UK & Ireland)

www.genealogy-guide.org.uk/adoption.html (Genealogy guide to obtaining adoption certificates)

www.adopteeconnect.com/p/a/5 (Irish adoption registry)

ARCHIVES, LIBRARIES, COLLECTIONS & RESOURCES (THE UK & IRELAND)

The Internet provides access to a variety of resources ranging from national and regional archives to collections held by organisations, businesses and individuals. The following entries list various UK and Irish resources by location and include a selection of websites found under subject headings. If your own area is not listed specifically, it can generally be found by typing the area or county name followed by the word 'records' into any Internet search engine.

GENERAL COLLECTIONS

www.britishpathe.com/ (Pathe News film archives)

www.newsreelarchive.com/ (General Newsreel Archives)

www.movietone.com/n_Index.cfm (Movietone News Archives)

www.movingimagesource.us/research/guide/132 (A list of moving image libraries and resources)

www.history.ac.uk/ (Institute of Historical Research Links)

en.wikipedia.org/wiki/List_of_film_archives (Wikipedia's International list of historical film archives)

www.britainfromabove.org.uk/ (Search for historic pictures of Britain from the air)

www.nationalarchives.gov.uk/search/quick_search.aspx (Search the National Archives)

www.york.ac.uk/inst/bihr/ (Website of the Borthwick Institute, York, which holds one of the biggest archive repositories outside London)

www.archives.org.uk/general/county-archive-research-network-carn.html (About CARN, the County Archive Research Network, and how to obtain a research ticket)

www.genuki.org.uk/search/ (Type the word 'archive' into Genuki's own search engine to obtain links to thousands of national and regional archive sources)

www.sog.org.uk/library/upper.shtml (Society of Genealogists' resources by subject)

www.archiveshub.ac.uk/ (Search for university and college archives)

copac.ac.uk/ (Access to online catalogues of major universities and national libraries in the UK and Ireland)

ds.dial.pipex.com/town/square/ac940/weblibs.html (Complete list of British libraries with contact details and catalogues of resources available to the researcher)

www.bl.uk/ (Facilities to search the British Library for genealogy items)

www.history.ac.uk/gh/lfguide.htm (List of guides to records held at the Guildhall Library)

www.genogold.co.uk/ (Genogold site of UK genealogical resources)

www.curiousfox.org.uk/ (UK village by village genealogical queries and answers)

www.old-picture.com/ (Free search for historic pictures on a wide range of subjects)

CHANNEL ISLANDS

www.bigenealogy.com/location/channel.htm (CI genealogy & history site)

www.familytreeforum.com/content.php/300-Channel-Islands (CI Family tree forum)

www.islandlife.org/genealogy_gsy.htm (Archives and other islands family history resources)

chi.genuki.weald.org.uk/ (Start your search here for Channel Islands genealogy, island by island)

www.genuki.org.uk/Societies/ChannelIslands.html (Genuki's list of Channel Islands Family History Societies)

ENGLAND

www.efdss.org/efdss-the-full-english (English folk dance & song archives)

www.britishcouncil.org/organisation/history/archives (British Council research)

independentlibraries.co.uk/ (Association of Independent Library holdings)

www.londonfhc.org/ (London Family History Centre)

www.genealogyinengland.com/index2.htm (Lots of links from Genealogy in England)

www.genuki.org.uk/big/eng/ (Start your search here for family tree resources for any English county)

www.genealogylinks.net/uk/england/ (Thousands of links specifically geared to English family history research)

genealogy.about.com/od/england/index.htm (Lots of English genealogy resources)

www.cousinconnect.com/p/a/0/s/ENGLISH (English genealogical postings, queries and contacts)

tinyurl.com/8qrpuej (London Metropolitan Archives (LMA))

www.westminster.gov.uk/archives/ (City of Westminster archives)

www.gunnerside.info/index.html (Extensive genealogical and other information for the areas of Gunnerside and Swaledale, North Yorkshire)

www.berksfhs.org.uk/cms/index.php (Berkshire Family History Society's links to general family history resources on the internet)

IRELAND (including NORTHERN IRELAND)

www.irishgenealogy.ie/en/ (Irish genealogy in Gaelige & English)

irisharc.org/ (Irish Ancestry Research Centre)

www.rootsireland.ie/ (Roots-Ireland web site)

www.genuki.org.uk/big/irl/ (Start your search here for family history information related to any Irish county)

tinyurl.com/34c3fyl (Northern Ireland General Register Office site with links to researching historical records)

www.genealogylinks.net/uk/ireland/index.html (Irish genealogical links and resources)

genforum.genealogy.com/ireland/ (Irish genealogy forum)

www.nationalarchives.ie/ (Site of The National Archives of Ireland)

www.originsnetwork.com/help/helpio-census1841.aspx (Irish strays 1841 census)

www.censusfinder.com/irish_surnames.htm (Irish clan and surname resources)

www.proni.gov.uk/ (Public Record Office of Northern Ireland)

www.irelandseye.com/aarticles/features/tracing3.shtm (Trace your roots anywhere in Ireland)

www.nationalarchives.ie/ (Irish National Archives)

www.genuki.org.uk/Societies/Ireland.html (Genuki's list of Irish Family History Societies)

www.ancestryireland.com/ (Ancestry Ireland website with ancestor search)
freespace.virgin.net/alan.tupman/sites/irish.htm (Lots of links to Irish passenger list sources)
www.finditireland.com/links/irishclansites.html (Links to individual Irish clan name sites)
en.wikipedia.org/wiki/Williamite_war_in_Ireland (Williamite–Jacobite War in Ireland)
www.rootsweb.com/~irlkik/ksurnam2.htm (County Kilkenny surname list)
www.irishgenealogy.ie (Search online Irish church records)

ISLE OF MAN

www.genuki.org.uk/big/iom/ (Start here for IOM family history resources)
www.genuki.org.uk/Societies/IsleOfMan.html (Genuki's list of Isle of Man Family History Societies)
www.genealogylinks.net/uk/england/isle-of-man/index.html (Lots of IOM genealogy links)
www.isle-of-man.com/manxnotebook/famhist/genealgy/chomes.htm (IOM children's homes)
www.bigenealogy.com/location/man.htm (IOM history and genealogy)
www.isle-of-man.com/manxnotebook/famhist/fhsjv12.htm (Index to Manx family history journal that can be read on your computer)
www.isle-of-man.com/manxnotebook/famhist/pregs/lnbu1718.htm (Isle of Man burials 1718–1793)
www.isle-of-man.com/manxnotebook/famhist/genealgy/intern.htm (POW camps on the Isle of Man)

ISLES OF SCILLY

www.cornwall-opc.org/Par_new/h_k/isles_of_scilly.php (Scilly Isles Parish website)
www.familytreeforum.com/content.php/298 (Scilly Isles genealogy forum)
www.iosmuseum.org/family.html (Isles of Scilly Museum, family history page)
www.genuki.org.uk/big/eng/Cornwall/IslesofScilly/index.html (Lots of Scilly Isles genealogy links)
freepages.genealogy.rootsweb.ancestry.com/~ricksmith61/scilly/wc_toc.html (Scillonian site, with genealogy links to information about individual families)
http://freepages.genealogy.rootsweb.ancestry.com/~ricksmith61/scilly/index.html (Rootsweb's Isles of Scilly page)

SCOTLAND

www.sctbdm.com/index.php (Free BMD resources)

tinyurl.com/ldvuwkv (Scottish immigrants and emigrants)

www.fifefhs.org/ (Fife Family History Society)

www.scotlandsfamily.com/ (Scotland's Family genealogy site)

www.workhouses.org.uk/Scotland/UnionsScotland.shtml (Scottish poorhouse and workhouse resources)

www.genuki.org.uk/big/sct/ (Start your search here for Scottish genealogy links)

www.scotlandspeople.gov.uk/content/help/index.aspx?r=1229 (Official Scottish genealogy site, with links to birth, marriage and death records, census and other information)

www.scan.org.uk/ (Scottish Archive network site)

www.gro-scotland.gov.uk/site-map.html (Scottish General Register Office site)

www.nas.gov.uk/ (National Archives of Scotland)

www.genuki.org.uk/Societies/Scotland.html (Genuki's list of Scottish Family History Societies)

www.scottishdocuments.com/ (Scottish genealogy document digitisation project)

www.nas.gov.uk/guides/inheriting.asp (An explanation of inheritance laws and procedures in Scotland)

www.bigenealogy.com/location/scotland.htm (Scotland's history and genealogy resources)

www.ancestor.abel.co.uk/links.html#pro (Miscellaneous Scottish family history links)

www.nas.gov.uk/guides/sheriffCourt.asp (Guide to Scottish Sheriff Court records)

www.electricscotland.com/argentina/index.htm (Scottish settlers in South America)

myweb.tiscali.co.uk/scotsinargpat/ (Scots in Argentina and Chile)

www.scotsorigins.com/ (Lots of Scottish resources including a search facility)

www.rampantscotland.com/genealogy.htm (Scottish genealogy by region)

www.oz.net/~markhow/scotsros.htm (Alphabetical list of Scottish Record Offices and Archives)

WALES & ANGLESEY

tinyurl.com/m9c9gfv (Common Words & Phrases on Welsh head stones & Memorial Inscriptions

www.welshgenealogy.net/ (New Welsh genealogy website)

www.genuki.org.uk/big/wal/ (Start your search here for Welsh genealogy resources)

www.archivesnetworkwales.info/ (Welsh archives network, with lots of links and resources) www.genuki.org.uk/Societies/Wales.html (Genuki's list of Welsh Family History Societies)

www.censusfinder.com/wales.htm (Comprehensive list of online census material for Wales and Anglesey)

www.genealogy-of-uk.com/Wales/Anglesey/genealogy.htm (Various Anglesey record sources)

www.genuki.org.uk/big/wal/CAE/Llandegai/Llandegai51.html (Complete transcription of 1851 census – Llandegai, Wales)

www.welshmariners.org.uk/ (Database of thousands of Welsh mariners)

www.theshipslist.com/pictures/welsh1.htm (Details about Welsh emigrants to Patagonia)

www.oz.net/~markhow/welshros.htm (Alphabetical list of Welsh Record Offices and Archives)

ARCHIVES, LIBRARIES, COLLECTIONS & RESOURCES (OVERSEAS)

Those who have ancestors that came from or went to other countries can gain access to a wide range of records on the internet. Below are some of the main websites. Other countries may be searched for using search engines such as Google, Yahoo etc. or by using the World Gen website listed below.

ALL COUNTRIES

www.worldgenweb.org/ (World Gen international genealogical project page)

freepages.genealogy.rootsweb.com/~northing/ethnic/index.html (Links to ethnic resources on the net)

www.afhs.ab.ca/aids/geographic/geog.html (Links to family history sources by country or region)

www.exploregenealogy.co.uk/GoingGlobalCategory.html (Guide to tracing ancestors abroad)

AFGHANISTAN

www.kindredtrails.com/afghanistan.html (Afghanistan Genealogy & Family History Resources)

AFRICA (See also alphabetical list for individual countries)

tinyurl.com/oqm7dlh (Central African Republic Genealogy Mailing List)
home.global.co.za/~mercon/ (African genealogy links, resources and search)
www.afrigeneas.com/ (African American genealogy)
tinyurl.com/cs8bm79 (African-genealogy forum)
society.searchbeat.com/africaroots.htm (African genealogy links)
www.jewishgen.org/safrica/ (Jewish genealogy in South Africa)
southafricanfamilyhistory.wordpress.com/ (Links to South African genealogy resources)
www.sephardicgen.com/nafrica_sites.htm (North African Sephardic genealogy)
www.cyndislist.com/africa.htm (Full listing of all African family history resources)

ALBANIA

www.rootsweb.ancestry.com/~albwgw/genealogy.html (Albanian GenWeb)
distantcousin.com/links/ethnic/albanian/ (Various resources)

ANDORRA

boards.tiscali.ancestry.co.uk/localities.weurope.andorra.general/mb.ashx (Andorra genealogical message board)

ARABIAN PENINSULAR

www.kindredtrails.com/oman.html (Oman National Resources)
www.qnl.qa/ (Qatar National Library page)
www.dnaancestry.ae/index_eg.php (Using DNA when researching Arab roots)
genforum.genealogy.com/uae/ (UAE genealogy forum)
genforum.genealogy.com/saudiarabia (Saudi Arabia genealogy forum)
www.kindredtrails.com/bahrain.html (Bahrain genealogy resources)
www.kindredtrails.com/kuwait.html (Kuwait genealogy resources)
tinyurl.com/7mnpu9m (Yemen genealogy)

ARCTIC & ANTARCTIC REGIONS (See also under CANADA)

www.jeffersonhosting.org/arctic-archives/ (Arctic Archives Project)
www.slawistik.hu-berlin.de/arcticarchives (International site)
tinyurl.com/qcrhejf (British Antarctic Survey Archives)

www.unlockingthearchives.rgs.org/themes/antarctica/ (Antarctica - Extreme Wilderness)

www.spri.cam.ac.uk/library/archives/ (The Thomas H. Manning Polar Archives)

ARMENIA

familysearch.org/learn/wiki/en/Armenia (Family history and genealogy)

ASCENSION ISLAND & TRISTAN DE CUNHA

www.archeion.talktalk.net/sthelena/familyhistory.htm (St Helena Institute page)

AUSTRALIA

trove.nla.gov.au/ (Australia's online National Library resources)

afhc.cohsoft.com.au/ (Australian Family History Compendium)

www.ihr.com.au/societies.html (Australian family history societies by state)

www.familybmd.com/australia.htm (Information, links and advice for tracing Australian ancestors)

www.familytreeforum.com/content.php/434-Australia (Forum with lots of useful links)

www.naa.gov.au/services/family-historians/index.aspx (National Archives of Australia genealogy page)

www.nla.gov.au/oz/genelist.html (Links to lots of Australian family history sites including official government resources)

www.coraweb.com.au/bdmau.htm (Search Australian Public Records online)

www.winthrop.dk/wc_toc.htm (Family tree of Captain Cook)

AUSTRIA

www.genealogylinks.net/europe/austria (Excellent selection of 70 Austrian genealogy links)

www.genealogylinks.net/europe/austria/cemeteries.htm (transcriptions of Austrian cemetery inscriptions + other links to BMD records)

search.ancestry.co.uk/Places/Europe/Austria/Default.aspx (Austrian resources at Ancestry.com)

AZERBAIJAN

search.ancestry.co.uk/Places/Europe/Azerbaijan/Default.aspx (Resources from Ancestry)

BALTIC STATES (ESTONIA, LATVIA & LITHUANIA)

www.genealoogia.ee/English/english.html (Estonian Genealogical Society)
www.aai.ee/~urmas/urm/vast.html (How to find relatives in Estonia)
www.rootsweb.ancestry.com/~lithuani/index.html (Lithuanian genealogy website)
www.rootsweb.ancestry.com/~ltuwgw (Links page to Lithuanian family history resources)
www.rootsweb.ancestry.com/~lvawgw (Latvian Genweb page)

BASQUE REGIONS

home.earthlink.net/~fybarra/ (Basque genealogy home page)
meilleursprenoms.com/site/regionaux/Basques/Basques.htm (Alphabetical list of Basque names)

BELARUS

www.belavtodor.belhost.by/eng/index.php?id=12 (Belarus Archives resources)
www.jewishgen.org/belarus/ (Jewish genealogy resources)

BELGIUM – also WALLOON & FLEMISH ANCESTRY

www.genealogylinks.net/europe/belgium/index.html (Links for tracing Belgian ancestry)
www.omniglot.com/writing/walloon.htm (Walloon language website)
olivetreegenealogy.com/hug/overview.shtml (Huguenot and Walloon ancestry)
www.genealogy-quest.com/collections/walloons.html (Walloon and French immigrants to Virginia 1621)

BENIN

tinyurl.com/luq6s8b (Rootsweb Benin Genealogy Mailing list)

BOLIVIA

en.geneanet.org/pays/research-genealogy-ancestry-Bolivia-BOL (Geneanet resources)

BOSNIA & HERZEGOVINA

www.farsarotul.org/nl16_1.htm (The Vlachs in Bosnia)
tinyurl.com/czpfdqk (Bosnia and Herzegovina message board)

www.genealogylinks.net/europe/bosnia_herzegovina/ (A wide range of Bosnia & Herzegovina genealogy links)

genforum.genealogy.com/bosnia/ (Bosnia/Herzegovina Genealogy Forum)

BURKINA FASO (Formerly Upper Volta)

http://tinyurl.com/mgxtkjo (Resources from Genealogy.com)

BURMA See under MYANMAR

CANADA

www.bac-lac.gc.ca/eng/Pages/default.aspx (National Archives & Library of Canada)

freespace.virgin.net/alan.tupman/sites/canada.html (Sites with Canadian genealogical source material)

jubilation.uwaterloo.ca/~marj/genealogy/thevoyage.html (Canadian immigration resources)

www.islandnet.com/~cghl/region.php?cat=Nova+Scotia (Canadian & Nova Scotia history & genealogy links)

www.accessgenealogy.com/country/canada.htm (Lots of Canadian resources)

www.accessgenealogy.com/test/canada.cgi (Canadian surname search)

www.rootsweb.com/~canmil/index.html (Canadian military history project)

www.bifhsgo.ca/ (Canadian site related to British Isles family history)

www.ubishops.ca/geoh/settlem/phases.htm (British settlement in the Eastern Townships 1820–1850, plus American and French settlers)

www.vpl.ca/ccg/History_Pioneers.html (Chinese pioneers in Canada)

freepages.genealogy.rootsweb.ancestry.com/~wjmartin/1886.htm (Records of Canadian accidental deaths and suicides in 1886)

www3.sympatico.ca/bkinnon/cemeteries.htm#can (Free online Canadian cemetery & burial records)

CANADA (Native Races including Inuit Eskimos & Metis)

tinyurl.com/kno8nhd (Inuit Arctic Council pages)

familysearch.org/learn/wiki/en/Canada_Native_Races (Native Canadian people studies)

www.native-languages.org/inuit_culture.htm (Native Alaskan Inuit /Eskimo cultural connections)

www.gov.ns.ca/nsarm/ (Nova Scotia Archives)

CARIBBEAN & WEST INDIES

grenadiangirl.wordpress.com/ (Grenada Genealogy links)
www.tc.umn.edu/~terre011/genhome.html (St Kitts & Nevis resources)
antiguamecomfrom.org/ (Antigua & Barbuda resources)
www.rootsweb.ancestry.com/~vctwgw/records.htm (St Vincent & Grenadines BMD & other records)
www.rootsweb.ancestry.com/~jamwgw/ (Rootsweb's Jamaican resources)
www.caribbeanroots.co.uk/Resources.html (Caribbean Ancestry and Heritage site)
www.movinghere.org.uk/galleries/roots/caribbean/caribbean.htm (Guide to tracing Caribbean roots)
genealogy.about.com/library/vital/blpuertorico.htm (Puerto Rico family history information)
www.sephardicgen.com/carib_sites.htm (Tracing record of Jews in the Caribbean)
www.candoo.com/genresources/#CAYMANS (Caymans genealogy links and resources)
www.indocaribbeanheritage.com/content/view/18/2/ (Indo-Caribbean Heritage resources)

CENTRAL AFRICAN REPUBLIC

tinyurl.com/oqm7dlh (Rootsweb Genealogical Mailing List)

CHINA

www.mandarintools.com/calendar.html (Convert Chinese calendar dates to their western equivalents)
www.yutopian.com/names/nametree.html (Find out about Chinese surnames and the regions they originate from)
www.rootsweb.com/~chnwgw/ (Chinese genealogy resources with listings by province)
eis.bris.ac.uk/~hirab/smp2.html (A website researching British members of the Shanghai Municipal Police 1854–1943)
www.vpl.ca/ccg/History_Pioneers.html (Chinese pioneers & Chinese/Canadian history)

CROATIA

www.croatia-in-english.com/ (Lots of genealogy & general Croatian links, in English)
www.about-croatia.com/croatian-names/ (Croatian genealogy and names)
genforum.genealogy.com/croatia/ (Croatian based genealogy forum)
www.appleby.net/genealogy.html (Very useful worldwide Croatian genealogy links including emigrants)

CUBA

www.cubagenweb.org/links.htm (Cuban genealogy links)
www.cubagenweb.org/ (Cuban genealogy centre)
genforum.genealogy.com/cuba/ (Cuba genealogy forum)
cubanfamily.iccas.miami.edu/ (Cuban genealogy project)
www.jewishvirtuallibrary.org/jsource/vjw/Cuba.html (Information and links regarding Jews in Cuba)

CYPRUS

genforum.genealogy.com/cyprus/ (Genealogy Forum)
boards.ancestry.com/topics.researchresources.vitals/3772/mb.ashx (Births, deaths and marriages registry contact details)

DAHOMEY (former) – (See under BENIN)

DENMARK

tinyurl.com/cm6ycvd (Danish emigration archives)
www.ddd.dda.dk/ddd_en.htm (Danish census resources)
www3.sympatico.ca/colin.swift/extr-rec.htm (Danish online family history resources)
www.genealogylinks.net/europe/denmark/ (over 100 Danish genealogy links)
genforum.genealogy.com/denmark/ (Denmark genealogy forum)

EGYPT

www.hsje.org/Genealogy.htm (Jews from Egypt specialist site)
tinyurl.com/cly8r5n (Egyptian Family history message board)

ESTONIA

tinyurl.com/mg9rhrc (Estonian resources from Family Search)
www.genealoogia.ee/English/english.html (Estonian Genealogy Society)

ETHIOPIA

http://tinyurl.com/lwja3tx (Genealogy message board for Ethiopia)

FINLAND AND ALAND ISLANDS

www.cyndislist.com/finland/newspapers/ (Finish newspaper links)
www.rootsweb.com/~finwgw/ (Resources for tracing your Finnish ancestors)
www.genealogylinks.net/europe/finland/ (Over 100 Finish & Aland Islands genealogy links)
www.rootsweb.ancestry.com/~finwgw/ (Finland Gen web site)
www.genealogia.fi/ (Genealogical Society of Finland)

FRANCE

tinyurl.com/c4aezmh (Links to online French resources)
france.worldvitalrecords.com/ (Search French family history sites here)
www.genealogylinks.net/europe/france/index.html (French genealogy resources)
www.theshipslist.com/ships/passengerlists/french_occupations1873.html (Old French occupations)
www.genealogy-quest.com/collections/walloons.html (Walloons and French who emigrated to Virginia 1621)

GEORGIA

feefhs.org/index.html (Federation of East European Family History Societies)
www.royalhouseofgeorgia.ge/royal-house/Genealogy (Royal House of Georgia genealogy)

GERMANY

www.genealogienetz.de/genealogy.html (German Genealogy Network)
german.about.com/library/weekly/aa020830a.htm (Links, tips and resources for researching German ancestors)
www.agfhs.org.uk/ (Anglo-German Family History Society)
homepages.rootsweb.com/~george/oldgermanprofessions.html (German occupations)
www.feldgrau.com/wsskb.html (German photographers in WWII)
www.cyndislist.com/germany.htm (Lots of resources from Cyndi's List)

GIBRALTAR

www.facebook.com/gibraltargenealogy (Gibraltar genealogy on Facebook)

www.familyhistory.com/surnames.asp?surname=Gibraltar&d=Gibraltar%20 genealogy (Resources from FamilyHistory.com)

www.interment.net/data/gib/trafalgar/index.htm (Names of people buried in Gibraltar 1798–1814)

www.gibraltargenealogy.com/ (Specialised Gibraltar family and general history site)

HUNGARY

www.rootsweb.ancestry.com/~wghungar/ (Map and research resources)

www.genealogia.hu/english/index.htm (Forum and web archive of Hungarian genealogy)

www.mol.gov.hu/?akt_menu=574&set_lang=466 (Website of National Archives of Hungary. Click top bar for translation in English)

www.genealogylinks.net/europe/hungary (Links to Hungarian genealogy resources)

genforum.genealogy.com/hungary (Genealogical discussion forum for Hungary)

ICELAND

genealogy.about.com/od/iceland/Iceland_Genealogy_sland_Ancestors.htm (Links and information)

genforum.genealogy.com/iceland/ (Iceland genealogy forum)

www.kindredtrails.com/iceland.html (Icelandic genealogy resources)

www.rootsweb.ancestry.com/~islwgw/ (Links to Iceland resources which in some cases date back to the 9th century)

INDIA

http://tinyurl.com/38zm5yq India Office Records at the British Library

www.genealogylinks.net/country/india/index.html (Lots of India & East India Company genealogy links)

indiafamily.bl.uk/UI/ (India Office web page)

genealogy.about.com/od/india/India.htm (Indian family history links)

www.indiaman.com/ (Colonial family connections in India – Magazine site)

valmayukuk.tripod.com/ (British India family history resources)

h.webring.com/hub?ring=britishindiafami (Links to miscellaneous sites with resources for Indian research)

ITALY

www.anglo-italianfhs.org.uk/ (Anglo-Italian Family History Society)

freespace.virgin.net/anglers.rest/Italianlinks.htm (Anglo-Italian FHS links)
www.genealogylinks.net/europe/italy (Lots of links and connections for Italian research)
lancione-laura.tripod.com/italian_genealogy_links.htm (US site with some interesting links)

JAPAN

www.samurai-archives.com/ (Samurai archives with genealogy link)
www.samurai-archives.com/clanindex.html (Clan family trees of Japanese families)
www.rootsweb.ancestry.com/~jpnwgw (Japan GenWeb)
www.distantcousin.com/Links/Ethnic/Japan.html (Distant cousins' site – Japanese resources)
www.familytreeforum.com/content.php/443-Japan (Forum and resources)

KAZAKHSTAN

www.genopro.com/genealogy-links/?country=KZ&t=Kazakhstan (Genealogy resources in Kazakhstan)

KOREA (North & South)

koreangenealogy.org/links/ (General Genealogy Links)
familysearch.org/learn/wiki/en/South_Korean_Family_History_and_Genealogy (Links and resources)
genealogy.inje.ac.kr/eng/main.htm (Inje genealogy library. Click 'English' tab for translation)
en.wikipedia.org/wiki/Korean_name (Understanding personal Korean names)

KYRGYZSTAN

www.zirs.uni-halle.de/projekte-northern-kyrgyzstan.php (Genealogy & History)

LATVIA

genforum.genealogy.com/latvia/ (Genealogy forum)
www.arhivi.lv/index.php?&319 (Latvian State Archives)

LIBERIA

lists.rootsweb.ancestry.com/index/intl/LBR/AFR-LIBERIA.html (Rootsweb's Liberia genealogy mailing list)

boards.tiscali.ancestry.co.uk/localities.africa.liberia/mb.ashx (Genealogy message board for Liberian family connections)

LIBYA

tinyurl.com/bw4gg6c (Libyan Family history message board)

LIECHTENSTEIN

kunden.eye.ch/swissgen/kibu/flkbinde.htm (A-Z of genealogical records)

LITHUANIA

www.lithuaniangenealogy.org/ (Lithuanian Global Genealogy)

search.ancestry.co.uk/Places/Europe/Lithuania/Default.aspx (Resources from Ancestry)

MADAGASCAR

www.genealogy.com/links/c/c-places-geographic,africa,madagascar.html (Genealogy.com resources)

MADEIRA (See under PORTUGAL)

MALAYSIA (See under SINGAPORE & MALAYSIA)

MALDIVES

www.rootsweb.ancestry.com/~mdvwgw/ (Maldives resources from Rootsweb)

MALTA

website.lineone.net/~mcgoa/malta2.html (Malta Registers at The National Archives)

www.genesreunited.co.uk/boards.page/board/genealogy_chat/thread/1148418
(Genes United Malta page)
www.maltafamilyhistory.com/ (Malta family history connections, mainly for British forces families)
www.barbsnow.net/Malta.htm (Guide to finding Maltese ancestors)

MARSHALL ISLANDS

tinyurl.com/plxxfar (Rootsweb genealogical mailing list)

MEDITERRANEAN REGION (General)

www.cyberpursuits.com/gen/mediterraneanlist.asp (Varied resources for Mediterranean and other regional research)

MEXICO

search.ancestry.co.uk/search/db.aspx?dbid=1771 (Search the 1930 Mexican census)
genforum.genealogy.com/mexico/ (Genealogy forum for those with Mexican ancestors)

MIDDLE EAST

www.genealogynation.com/middle-east/ (Middle East Genweb project)

MOLDOVA

search.ancestry.com/Places/Europe/Moldova/Default.aspx (Ancestry resources)

MONACO

genforum.genealogy.com/monaco/ (Genealogy Forum)
www.monte-carlo.mc/en/general/family-tree/ (Royal Family Tree)

MONTENEGRO (See under SERBIA & MONTENEGRO)

MYANMAR (Formerly BURMA)

www.rootsweb.ancestry.com/~mmrwgw/ (Part of the Asia Gen Network)

NAMIBIA

genforum.genealogy.com/namibia/ (Genealogy Forum)

NAURU (Formerly Pleasant Island)

www.abc.net.au/ra/pacific/places/country/nauru.htm (History & Resources)

NEW ZEALAND

natlib.govt.nz/collections/a-z/national-newspaper-collection (NZ newspaper archives)

search.ancestry.co.uk/Places/New%20Zealand/Default.aspx (NZ resources from Ancestry.com)

homepages.ihug.co.nz/~tonyf/ (Website dedicated to pioneers and early settlers in New Zealand)

freepages.genealogy.rootsweb.com/~ourstuff/ (A strange but very useful list of variable resources for New Zealand, including barmaid registrations!)

www.angelfire.com/az/nzgenweb/links.html (Lots of New Zealand genealogy links with some area-specific ones)

homepages.ihug.co.nz/~origins/nzgene.htm (More useful NZ genealogy links)

NORTH KOREA (See under KOREA)

NORWAY

www.myheritage.com/research/category-Norway/norway (Nordic records from MyHeritage)

expertgenealogy.com/free/Norway.htm (Free Norwegian genealogy resources)

www.facebook.com/NorwayGenealogy?cid=fb_grc_Norway (Norwegian resources on Facebook)

homepages.rootsweb.com/~norway/index.html (More Norwegian resources and links)

www.accessgenealogy.com/country/norway.htm (Lots of links to Norwegian records)

www.genealogylinks.net/europe/norway (Lots of Norwegian resources by region)

genealogy.about.com/od/norway/Norway_Genealogy_Norsk_Genealogi.htm (Links and tips on researching ancestors from Norway)

PACIFIC ISLANDS (General)

www.abc.net.au/ra/pacific/places/country/nauru.htm (Links to Pacific Islands profiles)

PALAU /BELAU (Formerly Carolines)

lists.rootsweb.ancestry.com/index/intl/PLW/PALAU.html (Rootsweb Mailing List)

PORTUGAL

www.portugueseancestry.com/genealogy/html/madeira_resource.cfm (Madeira resources)

www.portugueseancestry.com (Search for a Portuguese ancestor with links to family trees)

www.genealogylinks.net/europe/portugal/index.html (Over 70 Portuguese genealogy links)

genforum.genealogy.com/portugal (Forum for those with Portuguese ancestors)

RUSSIA

lostrussianfamily.wordpress.com/ (Finding lost Russian and Ukrainian families)

www.familytreeforum.com/showthread.php/45093-Russian-Genealogy (Russian genealogy forum)

www.genealogylinks.net/europe/russia/index.html (Lots of Russian genealogy resources, including census links)

www.ancestry.com/search/locality/dbpage.aspx?tp=3258&p=5189 (Russian resources at Ancestry.com)

ST HELENA

www.archeion.talktalk.net/sthelena/familyhistory.htm (St Helena Institute page)

www.genuki.org.uk/big/Helena.html (Residents of St Helena during Napoleon's imprisonment 1815–1821 with other related names)

SAN MARINO

www.rootsweb.ancestry.com/~itawgw/San_Marino/san_marino_index.html (GenWeb resources)

SCANDINAVIA (All Scandinavian countries)

www.scanfest.org/NGenealogy/genealogy.htm (Advice, tips and links)
www.familytreedna.com/public/scandinavianydna/ (Scandinavian DNA project)
www.cyndislist.com/scan.htm (Scandinavian and Nordic Family History links)
genealogy.about.com/od/scandinavia/Scandinavian_Countries.htm (Scandinavian
links categorised by country)

SERBIA & MONTENEGRO

feefhs.org/links/serbia.html (Serbia genealogy resources)
www.rodoslovlje.com/ (Serbian Genealogical Society)
tinyurl.com/cgnp9zq (Montenegro genealogy links)
www.genealogylinks.net/europe/serbia-montenegro (Variety of genealogical links for
Serbia & Montenegro)
www.cyndislist.com/easteuro.htm (Valuable resources for Serbia, Montenegro and other
areas of Eastern Europe)

SEYCHELLES

freepages.misc.rootsweb.ancestry.com/~barker/ (Free resources)
www.nation.sc/index.php?art=5403 (Seychelles National Archives)

SINGAPORE & MALAYSIA

genforum.genealogy.com/malaysia/ (Malaysian genealogy forum)
www.lds.org.sg/index.php/family/family-history-centre (Singapore Family History
Centre)
genforum.genealogy.com/singapore/ (Singapore genealogy forum)
www.myfareast.org/SingaporeMemorials/index.html (Cemetery and memorial
links)
www.kindredtrails.com/singapore.html (Singapore Genealogy page)

SLOVENIA

feefhs.org/links/Slovenia/frg-sgsi.html (Slovenian Genealogy Society page)
www.genealogylinks.net/europe/slovenia/ (Lots of useful links including lists of
landowners, message board and surname index)

SOUTH AFRICA

familyhistoryresearch.com.au/courses/IntroFamilyHistory/ch8_SthAfrica.htm
(Lots of genealogy links)
home.global.co.za/~mercon/ (Advice and resources for tracing South African roots)
www.1820settlers.com/ (A free website dedicated to the British settlers in South Africa in 1820, their descendants and researchers)
search.freefind.com/find.html?id=91621572&map=0&page=0&ics=1 (Resources and links for Victorian British settlers in Natal)
home.global.co.za/~mercon/ (General South African genealogy pages)

SOUTH AMERICA (General)

www.stanmer.eclipse.co.uk/latinam1.html (Genealogical research tips for South America)
www.sabrits.co.uk/ ('Brits in South America' database)
www.argbrit.org/ (British settlers in Argentina with name search)
www.theshipslist.com/pictures/welsh1.htm (Details about Welsh emigrants to Patagonia)
archiver.rootsweb.com/th/read/SOUTH-AM-EMI/2004-04/1081269374 (South America genealogy message board)
www.electricscotland.com/argentina/index.htm (Scottish settlers in South America)
myweb.tiscali.co.uk/scotsinargpat/ (Scots in Argentina and Chile)

SOUTH KOREA (See under KOREA)

SPAIN

www.genealogylinks.net/europe/spain/index.html (Lots of Spanish genealogy links)
www.kindredtrails.com/spain.html (Links, tips and resources for tracing Spanish ancestors)
www.sephardicgen.com/spain_sites.htm (Jewish genealogy links in Spain)
genealogy.about.com/od/surname_meaning/a/spanish_names-2.htm (About Spanish surnames)

SRI LANKA

www.genealogysrilanka.com / (Specialised Sri Lanka genealogy site)
www.rootsweb.com/~lkawgw/ (Sri Lankan genealogy website)
www.ceylondatabase.net/Genealogy.html (Sri Lanka links when the country was called Ceylon)
genforum.genealogy.com/srilanka (Sri Lanka genealogy forum)

SURINAME & NETHERLANDS ANTILLES

www.looking4kin.com/group/suriname-genealogy (Geni information page)

SWEDEN

tinyurl.com/c8jl5vy (Swedish records online)
genforum.genealogy.com/sweden/ (Swedish genealogy forum)
www.genealogylinks.net/europe/sweden (Lots of Swedish research links)

SWITZERLAND

kunden.eye.ch/swissgen/schweiz-en.html (Misc. Resources)
is.gd/FsQ9UU (Church Records)
www.cyndislist.com/switzerland (Cyndi's extended list of resources)

SYRIA

tinyurl.com/pbt2s7s (Lots of genealogy links from FamilyHistory.com)

TAJIKISTAN

www.genealogy.com/links/c/c-places-geographic,asia,tajikistan.html (General Resources)

THAILAND

familysearch.org/learn/wiki/en/Thailand (Thailand Genealogy & history sources)

TRISTAN DE CUNHA (See under St HELENA)

TURKMENISTAN

www.genealogy.com/links/c/c-places-geographic,asia,turkmenistan.html (General resources)

TUVALU (Formerly Ellice Islands)

lists.rootsweb.ancestry.com/index/intl/TUV/TUVALU.html (Genealogy Mailing List)

UKRAINE

www.archives.gov.ua/Eng/genealogia.php (Centre for Genealogical research)
search.ancestry.co.uk/Places/Europe/Ukraine/Default.aspx (Ancestry resources)

UZBEKISTAN

tinyurl.com/m7tp9eo (Dombrabad Jewish & non-Jewish burials)
www.genealogy.com/links/c/c-places-geographic,asia,uzbekistan.html (General Links)

UNITED STATES OF AMERICA

familysearch.org/learn/wiki/en/American_Indian_Genealogy (US Native Indian genealogy)
www.usa.gov/Citizen/Topics/History-Family.shtml (U.S. Government genealogy links and resources)
www.interment.net/us/index.htm (U.S. cemetery records)
www.censusfinder.com/ (Census finder)
www.rootsweb.com/~bifhsusa/ (USA site dedicated to British Isles Family History)
www.accessgenealogy.com/native/index.htm (Native American Indian tribe links)
skyways.lib.ks.us/kansas/genweb/pioneers/index.html (Kansas pioneers lists)
www.rootsweb.com/~mopionee/ (Early Missouri settlers)
www.cagenweb.com/cpl/ (Californian Pioneer Project web page)
spartacus-educational.com/USAEengland.htm (Site dedicated to English emigrants to the USA)

UPPER VOLTA (See under BURKINA FASO)

VATICAN

www.vatican.va/archive/ (Vatican Archives page)
en.wikipedia.org/wiki/Vatican_Secret_Archives (Wikipedia page containing lists of Cardinals & Prefects)

BIBLES, FAMILY

Contrary to popular opinion, the interest in family history is not a modern phenomenon and in the past some families would note births, marriages and deaths in their family bible. Many have been lost but there are now both individuals and groups of people intent on preserving the records that remain.

freepages.genealogy.rootsweb.ancestry.com/~familybibles/ (Family Bible website)
www.cyndislist.com/bibles.htm (Cyndi's List index to general bible resources)
www.ancestorhunt.com/family_bible_records.htm (Genealogy details extracted from family bibles)
www.complete-bible-genealogy.com/ (Genealogy of Biblical characters after whom your ancestor may have been named)
www.torrens.org.uk/BFB/ (British family bible resources)

BIRTHS, BAPTISMS, MARRIAGES, DIVORCES & DEATHS

Literally thousands of sites deal with these vital subjects and the associated subjects of baptism and burial. Most have links to each other and many can be found using the Comprehensive Genealogy Sites in the first section of this book. Below is a selection of general resources, together with some of the most useful websites in particular categories. In the listings there are also some obituary links. Most modern major newspapers now have internet-based obituary pages. To find them simply type the name of the newspaper into a search engine, followed by the word 'obituaries'.

tinyurl.com/bmzxp2j (Google's list of BMD sites)
www.gro-scotland.gov.uk/ (Scottish GRO)
www.genuki.org.uk/big/eng/CivilRegistration.html (Links and resources for civil registration in the UK and Ireland)
www.ukbmd.org.uk/genuki/reg/ (List of registration districts for England and Wales)
www.gro.gov.uk/gro/content/certificates/default.asp (Information on how to obtain certificates)

www.freebmd.org.uk/ (Free search through GRO birth, marriage and death indexes; check years available)

www.1901censusonline.com/bmd.asp?wci=BMDlanding&searchtype=10 (Search birth, marriage and death GRO indexes 1837–2004 for England and Wales)

homepage.ntlworld.com/hitch/gendocs/info_bmd.html (Guide to birth, marriage and death certificates available from the General Register Office for England and Wales)

www.familysearch.org/Eng/Search/frameset_search.asp (Gives free access to the LDS [Mormon] Church's vast family history collection of records of all religions, including the International Genealogical Index

freepages.genealogy.rootsweb.com/~hughwallis/IGIBatchNumbers.htm (How to search the IGI (*above*) using batch numbers)

www.ukbmd.org.uk/index.php (Links to lots of birth, marriage and death resources)

www.british-genealogy.com/forums/archive/index.php/f-167.html (Lists of unwanted birth, marriage and death certificates that may assist your genealogical research)

www.interment.net/uk/index.htm (British cemetery records)

www.familyrelatives.org/ (A site that claims to hold over 750 million records – viewable by subscription)

www.BMDindex.co.uk/ (Search for BM&D certificates 1837–2005 – fee payable)

www.cornwall-opc-database.org/searchdb.php?dbname=burials (Search for Cornish birth, death or marriage certificates)

www.genuki.org.uk/big/eng/YKS/Misc/Transcriptions/NRY/

www.proni.gov.uk/ (Site for the Public Record Office of Northern Ireland)

BAPTISMS

tinyurl.com/cvvqfxe (GENUKI list of regional baptism records)

www.cornwall-opc-database.org/searchdb.php?dbname=baptisms (Search for Cornish baptisms)

freespace.virgin.net/tt.indexes/Bapt01y+.pdf (PDF format online baptism records for Wiltshire)

www.genuki.org.uk/big/eng/SOM/Wellington/Transcripts/index.html#baptisms (Baptism records for Wellington, St John, Somerset 1683–1812)

BASTARDY EXAMINATIONS

tinyurl.com/bvs3n7q (GENUKI list of bastardy records)

www.ukat.org.uk/thesaurus/term.php?i=18631 (UKAT links to bastardy documents)

freepages.genealogy.rootsweb.com/~mrawson/brasted4.html (Some early bastardy records from Brasted, Kent)

BURIALS, CEMETERY, GRAVEYARD & CREMATORIUM RECORDS

tinyurl.com/d2acz55 (Thousands of UK cemetery resources)

www.findagrave.com/ (Lots of resources to help you find a grave)

www.findagraveinscotland.com/ (Find a grave in Scotland)

tinyurl.com/dxr3pn6 (Nationwide list of burial lists and indexes from GENUKI)

www.deceasedonline.com/ (Search registers by country, region, county, burial authority or crematorium free of charge)

www.interment.net/ (Cemetery records online worldwide, including cemeteries flooded when dams were constructed)

www.cwgc.org/ (Commonwealth War Commission's records)

www.srgw.demon.co.uk/CremSoc/LegalEtc/Archives.html (Archives of the Cremation Society)

www.rootsweb.com/~engcemet/ (England Tombstone Project – countrywide links)

www.gravestonephotos.com/index.php (Gravestone photograph archives listed by county and by surname)

www.isle-of-wight-memorials.org.uk/ (Isle of Wight memorials and monuments)

www.cornwall-opc-database.org/searchdb.php?dbname=burials (Search for Cornish burials)

www.sfhg.org.uk/mipageA.html (Index to burial names found in Suffolk)

www.haverhill-uk.com/pages/burial-records-137.htm (Burials at Haverhill)

www.isle-of-man.com/manxnotebook/famhist/pregs/lnbu1718.htm (List of 18th-century Isle of Man burials)

freepages.genealogy.rootsweb.com/~mrawson/gwichbur.html (List of Greenwich Burials, 1820–1821)

www.genuki.org.uk/big/eng/SOM/Wellington/Transcripts/index.html#burials (Burial records – Wellington St John, Somerset 1683–1812)

www.historyfromheadstones.com/index.php?home (Irish gravestones and graveyards)

www.interment.net/data/gib/trafalgar/index.htm (List of burials in Gibraltar, 1798–1814)

bacsa.frontisgroup.com/bin/index.php (European cemeteries in India)

www.interment.net/ (Graveyard transcriptions from around the world sorted by country)

BRASS MEMORIALS

www.medievalgenealogy.org.uk/sources/brasses1.shtml (Links to monumental brass resources)

www.mbs-brasses.co.uk / (Monumental brass memorials and engraved plates)

CERTIFICATES

ukbmd.org.uk/genuki/reg/regoff.htm (List of register offices where you can obtain certificates)

www.gro.gov.uk/gro/content (Information on how to obtain certificates)

www.cornwall-opc-database.org/searchdb.php?dbname=burials (Search for Cornish birth, death or marriage certificates)

www.british-genealogy.com/forums/archive/index.php/f-167.html (Unwanted birth, marriage and death certificates that are available to genealogists)

www.BMDindex.co.uk/ (B, M & D certificates, 1837 onwards – fee payable)

CORONERS COURTS (INQUESTS)

tinyurl.com/bmo5l3b (National Archives guide to obtaining inquest and coroners' records)

tinyurl.com/blansr9 (UK wide resources)

www.salford.gov.uk/living/bmd/historysearch/genealogy/coronerrecords.htm (Where to find Lancashire inquest records)

DIVORCE

tinyurl.com/br8f6ak (Search here for marriage and divorce records)

www.familyhistory.uk.com/index.php?option=com_content&task=view&id=548&Itemid=29 (UK guide to divorce records)

www.nas.gov.uk/guides/divorce.asp (Scottish guide to divorce records)

www.nationalarchives.gov.uk/catalogue/RdLeaflet.asp?sLeafletID=260 (Guide and index references to divorces before 1858 from The National Archives)

www.nationalarchives.gov.uk/catalogue/RdLeaflet.asp?sLeafletID=53 (Guide and index references to divorces after 1858 from The National Archives)

MARRIAGES

tinyurl.com/bukfsts (Marriage resources throughout the UK)

genuki.cs.ncl.ac.uk/StCathsTranscriptions/ (A selection of transcriptions from St Catherine's marriage Index up to 1861)

www.old-liverpool.co.uk/marriages.html (Liverpool marriages)

www.genuki.org.uk/big/eng/SOM/Wellington/Transcripts/index.html#marriages (Marriage records from Wellington St John, Somerset 1683–1783)

www.cornwall-opc-database.org/searchdb.php?dbname=marriages (Search for Cornish marriages) www.dur.ac.uk/j.m.hutson/tudhoe/md1696.html (Marriage Duty tax returns – Tudhoe, Durham 1696)

www.genuki.org.uk/big/eng/YKS/Misc/Transcriptions/YKS/PaversIndex.html (Paver's Marriage Licence extracts for Yorkshire 1567–1628)

www.genealogylinks.net/marriages/uk/england/isle-of-man.htm (Isle of Man marriages)

search.ancestry.co.uk/search/db.aspx?dbid=1636 (Search Gretna Green marriages online)

MARRIAGE LICENCE ALLEGATIONS

genuki.cs.ncl.ac.uk/DEV/DevonMisc/MarriageLicenses.html (Devon allegations)

www.genuki.org.uk/big/eng/GLS/Bristol/MarriageBonds1679.html (Bristol allegations)

search.ancestry.co.uk/search/db.aspx?dbid=28562 (London marriage allegations 1597–1700)

OBITUARIES

tinyurl.com/bsel6b6 (Links to UK wide obituaries)

archiver.rootsweb.com/th/index/ENGLISH-OBITS (Search Rootsweb's UK obituary-sharing message archives)

politics.guardian.co.uk/politicsobituaries/0,1441,562536,00.html (*Guardian* newspaper site for political obituaries)

catless.ncl.ac.uk/Obituary/ (Obituaries with links to other 'death' subjects)

www.old-liverpool.co.uk/marriages.html (Liverpool obituaries)

www.ancestry.co.uk/search/obit/?us&dbid=7545 (Search for US obituaries)

PARISH & REGIONAL RECORDS

tinyurl.com/chqt4nz (A wealth of parish registers to read online)

www.parishfinder.co.uk:8080/ (Parish finder with distance calculator/surrounding parishes and Chapman Codes)

www.genuki.org.uk/search/ (Type 'parish registers' into the search engine to obtain thousands of links to UK records)

prtsoc.org.uk/ (Web page of the Parish Register Transcription Society)

www.freereg.org.uk/search/index.htm (Search parish registers free)

www.parishregisters.co.uk (Selection of parish register transcripts)

www.parishregisteruklook-upexchange.co.uk/ (Parish register look-ups)
www.wirksworth.org.uk/REGS-02.htm (Derbyshire parish registers guide)
edenlinks.rootsweb.com/1gp/gerhard/INDEX.HTML (Cumberland parish record transcripts)
www.great-harwood.org.uk/about/people/Great%20Harwood%20people.htm (Wide range of genealogy documents for Great Harwood)
www.yesterdaysnames.co.uk/parishes.htm (Index of names found in old parish magazines – commercial site)
webs.lanset.com/azazella/cornish_database.html (Cornish records, transcripts and databases)
www.cornwall-opc-database.org/searchdb.php?dbname=baptisms (Search for Cornish baptisms)
www.york.ac.uk/inst/bihr/ (Website of the Borthwick Institute for Archives which holds one of the biggest archive repositories outside London)
www.moonrakers.org.uk/files.asp (Download Wiltshire parish records)
www.parkhouse.org.uk/transcr/tcontent.htm (Devon and Somerset parish register transcriptions)
www.genuki.org.uk/big/eng/SOM/Wellington/Transcripts/index.html#baptisms (Baptism records for Wellington St John, Somerset 1683–1812)

CARTULARIES, CHARTERS & HISTORIC PUBLIC RECORDS

Charters, the legal documents that recorded the conditions of grants of land, property or other rights, are in effect the old equivalent of the modern deed. Cartularies on the other hand are documentary records (including charters and title deeds) kept by monasteries and sometimes by lay establishments. Many have now been deposited at record offices. Though they do not directly link to family trees, some include names, locations and other details that are invaluable to those tracing early ancestry. Records of this kind for specific individual abbeys or cities should be searched for using Google or other search engine, or the British History Online website below.

CARTULARIES

archive.org/search.php?query=cartulary%20AND%20collection%3Aamericana (Read Cartularies online)
paleo.anglo-norman.org/cart.html (Cartularies, their uses and faults)
www.medievalwriting.50megs.com/word/monasticcart.htm (Monastic cartularies)

CHARTERS

tinyurl.com/br7veta (Misc. UK charters)
medievalwriting.50megs.com/word/charter2.htm (Royal Charters)

PUBLIC RECORDS

tinyurl.com/c4akocf (Genuki's links to misc. public records)
www.medievalgenealogy.org.uk/sources/public.shtml#rec (Links to medieval public records available online)
en.wikipedia.org/wiki/Anglo-Saxon_Chronicle (All about the Anglo-Saxon Chronicle)

CENSUS RETURNS

National census records that are so useful to family historians began in 1841 and have continued to be taken on a ten-yearly basis since that time, excluding 1941 during World War II. These are invaluable for tying down families to particular locations and in giving us such vital details as names, ages, occupations and places of birth. Censuses taken before 1841 have often not survived, and normally did not contain information useful for genealogical purposes – some transcriptions have been placed on the net. The release of census material has been governed by the 100-year-rule, although the 1911 census was released early following public demand and can be accessed on various sites by simply searching the Internet. The 1921 census is expected to be released to the public in 2022. As website contents are continually being updated you should consult the sites listed under COMPREHENSIVE GENEALOGY SITES & SEARCH ENGINES for the most up to date listings.

INTERNATIONAL

www.censusfinder.com/ (Expanding site to help you find censuses anywhere in the world)

PRE-1841 CENSUSES

www.scan.org.uk/knowledgebase/topics/census_topic.htm (Early censuses & quasi-censuses)
genuki.cs.ncl.ac.uk/DEV/DevonMisc/Pre-1841Census.html (Pre 1841 censuses in Devon)

www.kirkbymalham.info/KMI/malhamdale/rental.html (14th C. Kirkby Malham Manorial census)

www.sfhg.org.uk/pubs-14.html (SFHG index of early censuses)

edenlinks.rootsweb.com/1gp/RECORDS/CC/CCINDEX.HTM (Constable's census 1787, Westmorland only)

www.origins.org.uk/genuki/NFK/places/y/yarmouth/census1803.shtml (Names in the Great Yarmouth population census, 1803)

www.origins.org.uk/genuki/NFK/norfolk/census/pre1841.shtml (Pre-1841 Norfolk censuses)

www.domesdaybook.co.uk/ (Online Domesday Book with search facility)

UNDERSTANDING THE NATIONAL CENSUS

tinyurl.com/dytej5g (Lots of resources and information from Genuki)

www.nationalarchives.gov.uk/pathways/census/main.htm (Interesting illustrated online historical study entitled *1901: Living at the time of the census*)

genuki.cs.ncl.ac.uk/Transcriptions/DUR/CensusAbbrev.html (The most common abbreviations found in the census)

ENGLAND & WALES CENSUSES FROM 1841

www.ukcensusonline.com (All censuses from 1841–1911 including transcripts and images)

www.freecen.org.uk/ (Free census records online)

www.nationalarchives.gov.uk/census / (National Archives' free search, pay to view)

www.1901censusonline.com/census.asp?wci=landing&searchtype=12 (Search all censuses 1841–1911)

www.genuki.org.uk/big/census_place.html (Search and locate places mentioned in the 1891 census)

1901census.rootschat.com/ (Private contributions from 1901 census with links)

www.1911census.co.uk (1911 census online)

www.apex.net.au/~tmj/c81-adrs.htm (Aids to finding an address in the 1881 census)

SPECIFIC LOCATIONS

www.genuki.org.uk/search/ (Search here for census records for your own region)

IRISH CENSUS

www.censusfinder.com/ireland.htm (Irish census records)
www.rootsweb.com/~fianna/guide/census.html (All about Irish census records and substitutes)
www.census.nationalarchives.ie (Irish censuses, fragments and substitutes)

SCOTTISH CENSUS

tinyurl.com/cu8mjlh (Ancestry's list of Scottish censuses)
scotlandspeople.gov.uk (Official site, links to Scottish census 1841–1901)
www.censusfinder.com/scotland.htm (Scottish census resources)

CHARITIES, INSTITUTIONS & THE POOR

Most towns, and even villages, had their own charitable institutions, such as almshouses and orphanages and, of course, workhouses. The latter were part of the Poor Law system, which also created records of, for instance, settlement and removal. The records that survive have usually been deposited at local archives, record offices and libraries. Because they will often be listed under their local names on the Internet, it may be necessary to search for them individually. For Asylums, see under **Hospitals and Asylums**.

ALL INSTITUTIONS

tinyurl.com/bp279et (Hundreds of Poor Law union records)
www.workhouses.org.uk/ (Site dedicated to workhouses, institutions and the poor)
www.old-liverpool.co.uk/snippets.html (Page with links to Liverpool institutions)
www.genuki.org.uk/big/eng/LIN/Caistor/caistor_union_list.txt (Caistor Poor Law Guardians and actual records 1836–1846)
archive.org/stream/mayhewslondonbei00mayhuoft#page/n7/mode/2up
(Read Mayhew's classic Victorian book about the London poor, online)

ALMSHOUSES / CHARTERHOUSES

tinyurl.com/csd28u4 (UK Charterhouse records – Search here also for Almshouses)
en.wikipedia.org/wiki/List_of_almshouses_in_the_United_Kingdom (List of UK almshouses with information links)

www.historyfish.net/clay/clay_hospitals.html (Medieval almshouses and hospitals)

BOARDS OF GUARDIANS (POOR LAW)

tinyurl.com/chscly6 (Lots of UK Board of Guardians links)
search.ancestry.co.uk/search/db.aspx?dbid=1557 (London Guardians and other Poor Law records)
www.batharchives.co.uk/what_we_hold/board_of_guardians_records/board_of_guardians.aspx (City of Bath records)
www.rascal.ac.uk/index.php?CollectionID=197&navOp=locID&navVar=24 (Irish records)
www.aberdeencity.gov.uk/education_learning/local_history/archives/loc_poorreliefrecords.asp (Aberdeen records)
www.wirksworth.org.uk/BOARD.htm (Derbyshire Board of Guardians members)
www.genuki.org.uk/big/eng/LIN/Caistor/caistor_union_list.txt (Caistor Poor Law Guardians and actual records 1836–1846)

BRITISH HOME CHILDREN (See under CHILD MIGRANTS)

FOUNDLINGS

tinyurl.com/bqp5h3a (Misc. links to records mentioning foundlings)
www.foundlingmuseum.org.uk/collections/research-resources/ (Foundling Hospital Museum website)
www.bbc.co.uk/radio4/womanshour/27_05_02/tuesday/info3.shtml (Listen online to a broadcast about abandoned babies)
www.24hourmuseum.org.uk/exh_gfx_en/ART28219.html (Love tokens left for foundlings, adding a pleasant note to otherwise sad stories)
www.bbc.co.uk/history/british/victorians/foundling_01.shtml (BBC account of Coram's Foundling Hospital)
www.ibdna.com/articles/Foundlings.htm (Using DNA in foundling cases)

ORPHANS, WAIFS & STRAYS

tinyurl.com/c2jyexh (UK orphanage records & resources)
www.orphanage.org/ (Links to international modern orphanages)
tinyurl.com/3r5yfzo (Dr Barnardo's Family History pages)

www.victorianlondon.org/dickens/dickens-charities.htm (List of names and addresses of Victorian London charities)

www.hiddenlives.org.uk/index.html (Lots of resources for researching orphans and waifs and strays including photos, documents and case files)

homepage.ntlworld.com/jeffery.knaggs/Instuts.html (Institutions in 1901 census, with some lists of residents)

www.isle-of-man.com/manxnotebook/famhist/genealgy/chomes.htm (Children's homes in the Isle of Man)

www.met-cityorphans.org.uk/history/archive.php (Details of the Metropolitan and City Police Orphanage archives)

homepage.ntlworld.com/jeffery.knaggs/I0012a.html (Orphanage of Mercy, Randolph Gardens, Kilburn, Paddington, London, 1901)

homepage.ntlworld.com/jeffery.knaggs/I0012c.html (St Vincent's Home for Desolate Roman Catholic Male Children, Paddington, 1901)

homepage.ntlworld.com/jeffery.knaggs/I0012d.html (Victoria Orphanage, Shirland Road, Paddington, 1901)

homepage.ntlworld.com/jeffery.knaggs/I0033f.html (National Industrial Home for Crippled Boys, Wrights Lane, Kensington, 1901)

homepage.ntlworld.com/jeffery.knaggs/I0096k.html (Sisters of Charity of St Vincent de Paul, Carlisle Place, Westminster, 1901)

homepage.ntlworld.com/jeffery.knaggs/I0106c.html (All Saints Home, 74–83 Margaret Street, Marylebone, 1901)

homepage.ntlworld.com/jeffery.knaggs/I2392a.html (Homes for Pauper Children Beaufort and Summerhill Roads, St George, Bristol, 1901)

homepage.ntlworld.com/jeffery.knaggs/I2364b.html (Staff and boys at the Home for Boys of the Bristol Union, Bristol, 1901)

homepage.ntlworld.com/jeffery.knaggs/I0109c.html (St Vincent De Paul's Convent and Orphanage, 9 Lower Seymour Street, Portman Square, Marylebone, 1901)

www.berksfhs.org.uk/journal/Dec2002/OrphansAtBearwood.htm (Orphans at Bearwood, the Merchant Seamen's Orphan Asylum, with pictures)

www.liverpool-genealogy.org.uk/Information/orphanages.htm (Names and details from Liverpool orphanage records)

REFUGES

inacityliving.piczo.com/?g=51055098&cr=7 (Facts and photos of the Ann Fowlers Women's Refuge, Everton)

tinyurl.com/ctag7sr (Information about, and photo of, Urania Cottage refuge, London) homepage.ntlworld.com/jeffery.knaggs/I2387a.html (List of those at the Bath Road Refuge for Penitent Women, Bristol, 1901)

SCHOOLS FOR THE DISABLED

ssa.nls.uk/film.cfm?fid=3396 (Amateur film profiling the Special School for disabled children at Fairmuir, Dundee)
www.nationalarchives.gov.uk/records/looking-for-place/school.htm (Search for schools in The National Archives)

SETTLEMENT & REMOVAL ORDERS

tinyurl.com/d6tveoy (Settlement Order discussion forum)
tinyurl.com/ccb94a7 (Settlement papers, etc, nationwide)
freepages.genealogy.rootsweb.com/~mrawson/brasted1.html (Some Kent settlement and removal order listings)
freepages.genealogy.rootsweb.com/~mrawson/removals.html (Index of over 500 appeals against removal orders in West Kent 1758–1788)

TRAMPS & VAGRANTS

www.wirksworth.org.uk/Board-2.htm#44 (Lists of Victorian tramps and vagrants in Derbyshire, plus other records)
www.workhouses.org.uk/WestLondon/WestLondonVagrants1848.shtml (List of London vagrants 1848)
www.sussexrecordsociety.org/pllistyearrecords.asp?an=&ap=&ld=1602 (Sussex vagrants)
www.legislation.gov.uk/ukpga/Geo4/5/83 (Vagrancy Act 1824 explained)

WORKHOUSES & POOR LAW RELIEF

tinyurl.com/c8abccx (GENUKI's national workhouse links)
www.genuki.org.uk/search/ (Type in the words POOR LAW into this search engine to find almost 8,000 links to Poor Law resources throughout Britain and the UK)
www.workhouses.org.uk/ (Website devoted to all aspects of the subject of workhouses and the poor)
www.nationalarchives.gov.uk/documentsonline/workhouse.asp (Workhouse correspondence files at the National Archives)

After the Poor Law Amendment Act of 1834, poor Victorian families received no money directly. If they needed help they had to go to the dreaded workhouse.
© 2014 Colin Waters Collection

www.nas.gov.uk/guides/poor.asp (Records of the poor in the Scottish National Archives)
homepage.ntlworld.com/jeffery.knaggs/l1549a.html (Staff and residents at North Witchford Union Workhouse, Doddington, Cambridgeshire in 1901)
www.stevebulman.f9.co.uk/cumbria/carlisle_workhouse_f.html (List of Carlisle workhouses)
www.sussexrecordsociety.org.uk/plhome.asp?an=&ap= (Database of Poor Law records in West Sussex)
www.genuki.org.uk/big/eng/LIN/Boston/boston_union_list.txt (Boston, Lincolnshire, Poor Law records from 1837 onwards)
www.genuki.org.uk/big/eng/LIN/Stamford/stamford_union_list.txt (Stamford Poor Law records 1835–1838)

www.genuki.org.uk/big/eng/YKS/Misc/Transcriptions/NRY/PickeringWorkhouse Index.html (Residents of Pickering Workhouse, Yorkshire, searchable by name, 1800s and 1900s)

www.genuki.org.uk/big/eng/LIN/poorhouse.html (List of Lincolnshire poorhouses and almshouses)

CHRONOLOGY

Knowing the chronology of events adds understanding to our family tree research, placing our ancestors firmly within an historical framework. For instance, knowing the years when a king or queen reigned or how to read dates written in Roman numerals on an old document helps us to date events exactly. There are a number of online aids.

AGE CALCULATOR

www.census-helper.co.uk (Calculate birth year from given age at any census)

CALENDARS, DATES & SAINTS' DAYS

www.hf.rim.or.jp/~kaji/cal/index.html (Examine any calendar from 1582 to the year 3000)

www.cslib.org/CalendarChange.htm (Researchers guide to the old and new style calendars)

www.combs-families.org/combs/reference/regnal.htm (A list of regnal years)

www.catholic.org/saints/stindex.php (Saints and Saints' Days listed alphabetically)

www.chsbs.cmich.edu/Kristen_McDermott/ENG235/EM_calendar.htm (Early modern calendar with Saints' Days and Festivals)

www.medievalgenealogy.org.uk/cal/medcal.shtml (A medieval calendar)

www.genuki.org.uk/big/easter/ (Lists the dates for Easter Sunday 1550–2049 and links to a calendar for each of those years)

medievalist.net/calendar/months.htm (Online calendar – click to find saints linked to any date)

EVENTS

www.thebookofdays.com/calender.htm (Click any date to find the historical links and events connected to that date throughout history)

www.angelfire.com/de/BobSanders/TIME1.html (Historical events AD 122 –1500)
www.angelfire.com/de/BobSanders/TIME2.html (ditto 1501–1900)
www.angelfire.com/de/BobSanders/TIME3.html (ditto 1900–1995)
www.history-timelines.org.uk/events-timelines/14-american-history-timeline.htm
(U.S. timeline)

FOREIGN NUMERALS

Often gravestones and inscriptions in the UK contain dates in foreign scripts. The following websites will help decipher them.

http://www.onlineconversion.com/roman_numerals_advanced.htm (Easily convert Roman numbers, dates, etc.)
www.alfabetos.net/japanese/japanese-numbers/learn-japanese-numbers-ordinals.php (Japanese numerals)
www.mandarintools.com/numbers.html (Traditional Chinese, Formal and simplified numerals)
easycalculation.com/funny/numerals/armenian.php (Armenian numbers)
en.wikipedia.org/wiki/Georgian_numerals (Understanding Georgian numerals)

CLANS

A clan is defined as a group of people united by kinship or descent from a common ancestor. Clans exist in many countries and more can be learned about them from the various websites listed below.

ALL CLANS WORLDWIDE

tinyurl.com/c5u5qxj (Genuki's clan links)
en.wikipedia.org/wiki/Clan (Explanation of clan systems, together with links throughout the world by country)
www.censusfinder.com/irish_surnames.htm (Irish clan and surname resources)
www.finditireland.com/links/irishclansites.html (Links to individual clan websites)
www.electricscotland.com/familytree/newsletters/index.htm (Links to clans and clan societies by name)
www.scotweb.co.uk/clans (Clans, kilts and tartans)
en.wikipedia.org/wiki/Scottish_clan (Scottish clans and clan map)
www.samurai-archives.com/clanindex.html (Family trees of Japanese clan names)

COATS OF ARMS, HERALDRY, EMBLEMS & FLAGS

It should be remembered that coats of arms, contrary to popular opinion, were not issued to a family name, but instead to an individual person and his descendants. Consequently, a number of people with the same surname will have different coats of arms and not everyone with that surname will be entitled to use those arms. Also listed below are some sites with resources for identifying flags, tartans and similar visual emblems.

FLAGS

www.anbg.gov.au/flags/semaphore.html (Flag Semaphore System)
www.anbg.gov.au/flags/signal-flags.html (International Marine Flags)
en.wikipedia.org/wiki/Lists_of_flags (Guide to world flags)
flagspot.net/flags/ (World flags reference site)

HERALDRY / COATS OF ARMS

www.heraldryaustralia.org/ (Australian Heraldry Society)
www.lyon-court.com/lordlyon/CCC_FirstPage.jsp (The Court of the Lord Lyon – the official heraldry office for Scotland)
www.nli.ie/en/heraldry-introduction.aspx (The Office of the Chief Herald of Ireland)
www.heraldik.se/artiklar/riks1.html (National Herald Board of Sweden)
onroerenderfgoed.ruimte-erfgoed.be/Default.aspx?tabid=14705&language=en-US (Flemish heraldry)
www.college-of-arms.gov.uk/Faq.htm (All the answers you will need to questions about coats of arms and what arms have been granted to various families)
www.ihgs.ac.uk/ (Website of the Institute of Heraldic and Genealogical Studies)
www.heraldica.org/topics/glossary/ (Miscellaneous heraldic study links with glossary and dictionaries)
www.cyndislist.com/heraldry.htm#General (Lots of heraldry resources)
www.theheraldrysociety.com/ (Website of the Heraldry Society)
www.heraldry-scotland.co.uk/ (Scottish Heraldry Society site)
www.leitrim-roscommon.com/heraldry/heraldry.html (Gaelic Irish heraldry site)
www.heraldry.ca/ (Royal Heraldry Society of Canada)
www.digiserve.com/heraldry/ (Commercial site with links to free heraldry resources on the Internet)

COPYRIGHT

Copying or using pictures and documentation of others when compiling family trees and on personal genealogical websites is subject to the laws of copyright. Often simply asking the owner for written permission will solve any problems. Sometimes the owner is not known or the original is very old and then further advice is needed.

www.copyrightservice.co.uk/copyright/p01_uk_copyright_law (UK copyright law)
www.learncopyright.co.uk/demo (Interactive website explaining UK copyright)
www.ict4lt.org/en/en_copyright.htm (General guidelines on copyright)

DIRECTORIES

Directories provide valuable information, especially trade directories which give business names and addresses and quite often home addresses also. Because they were published on a regular basis, they can help family historians not only locate their ancestor's business but also determine the years the business was in operation. Changes of location or name are also useful as an aid to estimating the date of death or retirement of proprietors. Most public libraries now have collections of these old local directories. Others can often be located on the Net.

www.familyrelatives.com/search/search_pigots_books.php (Search Pigot's directories online)
digital.nls.uk/directories / (Scottish Post Office directories)
www.historicaldirectories.org/ (Trades directories for the UK; search by location, decade or keyword)
www.genuki.org.uk/search/ (Type the word 'directory' into the search engine to find thousands of trade and other directory resources for the UK and Ireland)

DNA/GENETIC GENEALOGY

To be at the cutting edge of ancestor research, DNA and genetics can be used to trace not only your ancestors but also your family's historic geographical origins.

tinyurl.com/d6x3faz (Links to lots of DNA genealogy related sites)
www.dnaancestryproject.com/ (Using DNA and genetics to trace your family tree)
www.ramsdale.org/adam.htm (Genetics and genealogy – technical articles)

www.scotsfamily.com/genetic-genealogy.htm (Genetic genealogy for Scotland)
www.cambridgedna.com/genealogy-dna-genetic-genealogy.php (Cambridge DNA services for discovering genetic heritage)
www.ibdna.com/articles/Foundlings.htm (Using DNA in foundling and abandoned child cases)

DOMESDAY BOOK

The invasion of Britain in 1066 by William the Conqueror changed the face of Britain forever. The changes in land ownership and the census of the land in 1086 gave us the 'Domesday Book', a collection of over 13,000 individual records listing landowners, previous landowners and their social status, as well as their possessions at that time.

www.nationalarchives.gov.uk/domesday/ (National Archives Domesday Book page with search facility)
www.domesdaybook.co.uk/ (Online Domesday Book with search facility)

EDUCATION

Educational records can be difficult to locate on the Internet, though school addresses, pictures, lists of staff and sometimes pupils can increasingly be found. A good tip is to try typing the name of the particular school in question or the education authority you are seeking into a search engine. Often this will bring up obscure websites or educational resources which do not appear on the major genealogy sites.

www.genuki.org.uk/search/ (Type 'school' or 'schools' into this search engine to access thousands of educational documents and resources)
tinyurl.com/c9j5hap (Thousands of education related links)
tinyurl.com/dyj7deu (Google's list of genealogy related school and other educational links)
www.genuki.org.uk/big/eng/YKS/Misc/Transcriptions/NRY/CroptonSchool Register.html (Cropton School registers)
www.nas.gov.uk/guides/education.asp (Guide to Scottish education records)
homepage.ntlworld.com/jeffery.knaggs/l0142c.html (Residents of Home and Colonial Training College, Grays Inn Lane, St Pancras, London, 1901)
homepage.ntlworld.com/jeffery.knaggs/l1167b.html (Staff in residence at Royal Holloway College, Egham, Surrey, in 1901 census)

homepage.ntlworld.com/jeffery.knaggs/I1170c.html (Staff and boys at Beaumont College, Priest Hill, Egham, Surrey, in 1901 census)

homepage.ntlworld.com/jeffery.knaggs/I2370b.html (Staff and boys at the Clifton Certified Industrial School for Boys, Church Path, Clifton Wood, Bristol, in 1901 census)

www.history.ac.uk/gh/christ1.htm (Guide to Guildhall records of the 'Bluecoat Schools')

www.hertfordshire-genealogy.co.uk/data/education/schoolsandecucation.htm (Old photographs of Hertfordshire schools)

www.genuki.org.uk/big/eng/DBY/Newbold/SchoolMasters.html (List of Newbold, Derbyshire, school teachers 1818–1887)

met.open.ac.uk/genuki/big/eng/BKM/Aylesbury/schools/grammar.html (Names associated with Aylesbury Grammar School 1678–1903)

www.kirkbymalham.info/KMI/kirkbymalham/kmfgschool.html (Website of Kirkby Malham Grammar School, with list of schoolmasters 1736–1873)

www.hertfordshire-genealogy.co.uk/data/education/stalbans-schools.htm (St Albans' 19th-century school staff)

ELECTION RECORDS

For those who had ancestors involved in the political processes, there are a number of sources available on the Internet. Many are small documents listing voters or those eligible to vote in particular areas. As they are too numerous to list individually, they should be searched for specifically using a search engine such as Google. Poll books (1690–1872) show how individuals voted and where they lived. If they had property in different parts of the county, certain people may be found listed more than once. Some poll books also contain speeches and statements written by candidates for election. Electoral registers date from 1832 to the present day, listing all those eligible to vote.

ELECTIONS, ELECTORAL ROLLS & REGISTERS

tinyurl.com/c5phy32 (National Archives' advice on searching for electoral records)

tinyurl.com/lcwzbj (Electoral Register resources in the British Library)

www.genuki.org.uk/search/ (Search here for lists of electors from your own area using the words 'electors' or 'electoral roll' in the search box)

www.british-history.ac.uk/search.asp?query1=elections (List of historic records concerning British elections from early times)

www.origins.org.uk/genuki/NFK/norfolk/voting/ (Links to documents concerning Norfolk voting registers)

www.celticcousins.net/ireland/galway1727.htm (Galway election list 1727)

POLL BOOKS

www.genuki.org.uk/search/ (Enter the words 'poll books' for links to over 500 resources with poll book references throughout the UK and Ireland)

archive.org/details/pollbooksccount00enggoog (Northumberland poll books)

archive.org/details/pollfortwoknigh00enggoog (Norfolk Knights poll book)

EMIGRATION & IMMIGRATION

When individuals and sometimes whole families settled in other countries, it can cause problems in tracing them. The documentation involved in their movements can, however, often lead a family historian on the road to finding them in a new location quite quickly. A number of family history sites and societies have transcribed some of these documents, making the task of finding them much easier – see also under **SHIPPING**.

CHILD MIGRANTS (INCLUDING BRITISH HOME CHILDREN)

tinyurl.com/lyptvw7 (Search the Canadian Archives for British Home Children)

www.automatedgenealogy.com/uidlinks/BhcList.jsp (Alphabetical listing linked to the 1901 census regarding the British Home Children)

freepages.genealogy.rootsweb.ancestry.com/~britishhomechildren/ (British Home Children register)

tinyurl.com/8xs2bm7 (Australian child migrants)

www.childmigrantstrust.com/ (Site dedicated to the compulsory migration of children from Britain to Australia, Canada and other parts of the Commonwealth)

www.bbc.co.uk/radio4/history/child_migrants.shtml (Listen to BBC broadcasts online regarding these child migrants)

ist.uwaterloo.ca/~marj/genealogy/homeadd.html (Young immigrants to Canada with links)

www.barnardos.org.uk/who_we_are/history/child_migration.htm (Barnardo's child migrant site)

www.goldonian.org/barnardo/child_migrationl.htm (Child migration history timeline)

EMIGRANTS / IMMIGRANTS

www.argbrit.org/ (British settlers in Argentina and Uruguay)

www.bytown.net/scots.htm (Emigration from Scotland in the 1800s to Glengarry County, Ontario and Lanark County, Ontario)

www.genuki.org.uk/search/ (Type the words 'emigrant' or 'immigrant' into the search engine to find hundreds of resources – try also 'emigrants' or 'immigrants' for a different set of records)

nationalarchives.gov.uk/search (type 'emigration' or 'immigration' into the search engine for many links and resources)

www.castlegarden.org/ (Offers free access to an extraordinary database of information on 10 million immigrants to the USA 1830–1892)

www.ellisisland.org/search/index.asp (Search thousands of names of immigrants that arrived at Ellis Island, New York, USA)

www.glaniad.com/stories.php?lang=en&t=2&storyId=34273 (Details about Welsh emigrants to Patagonia)

homepages.ihug.co.nz/~tonyf/ (Website dedicated to pioneers and early settlers in New Zealand)

www.eggsa.org/arrivals/eGGSA%20Passenger%20Project.html (South Africa resources)

www.ubishops.ca/geoh/settlem/phases.htm (British settlement in the Eastern Townships 1820–1850 plus American and French settlers)

www.abdn.ac.uk/emigration/user-guide.html (Database of Scottish emigrants)**NATURALIZATION RECORDS**

www.nationalarchives.gov.uk/records/looking-for-person/naturalised-britons.htm (UK advice sheet from The National Archives)

www.archives.gov/genealogy/naturalization/ (US nationalisation archives)

nationalarchives.gov.uk/search (Type 'naturalization' into the search engine for information and record sources)

www.ancestry.co.uk/search/db.aspx?dbid=3826 (Search Minnesota, USA, naturalization records 1854–1957; commercial site)

naturalizationrecords.com/canada/ (Canadian naturalisation records and related documents)

www.naa.gov.au/collection/explore/migration/naturalisation.aspx (Australian records)

www.movinghere.org.uk/galleries/roots/jewish/perspectives/perspectives.htm (Jewish naturalisation record links)

FAMILY HISTORY SOCIETIES & FAIRS

Family History Societies, known in genealogical circles as FHS's, form perhaps the largest and fastest growing interconnected social membership group in Britain, and indeed the world. Members collect and exchange information, as well as compiling books, lists and pamphlets regarding their own areas of interest. Lots of these are available for sale whilst others are put on the web for free consultation. Most FHS's are members of the Federation of Family History Societies (FFHS), though this is not always the case. Therefore it is always worth checking with your local library or telephone directory to see if smaller local groups are meeting in your own area or in the region that you are researching.

www.ffhs.org.uk/members2/contacting.php (FFHS website – find a Family History Society in your area or in Australia, Canada, New Zealand & USA)
www.genuki.org.uk/Societies/ (Genuki's links to foreign and specialist FHS's)
www.genuki.org.uk/Societies/England.html (Genuki's list of English Family History Societies listed by county)
www.genuki.org.uk/Societies/Wales.html (Genuki's list of Welsh Family History Societies)
www.genuki.org.uk/Societies/Scotland.html (Genuki's list of Scottish Family History Societies)
www.genuki.org.uk/Societies/IsleOfMan.html (Genuki's list of IOM Family History Societies)
www.genuki.org.uk/Societies/Ireland.html (Genuki's list of Irish Family History Societies)
www.genuki.org.uk/Societies/ChannelIslands.html (Genuki's list of Channel Islands Family History Societies)
/www.ffhs.org.uk/members2/onename.php (Guild of One-Name Studies website)
ne-name.org (Find a One-Name Society researching your own family surname)

FAMILY HISTORY FAIRS

geneva.weald.org.uk/ (Updated list of genealogical events and activities)
www.familyhistoryfairs.org/dateloc.html (More fairs)

FIRE INSURANCE

Insurance documents and certificates provide names, addresses and details of the property insured, all of which can give family historians an insight into their ancestor's background and lifestyle whether on a business or personal footing.

tinyurl.com/kzx4pfx (Fire insurance and similar documents at The National Archives)
www.history.ac.uk/gh/fire.htm (How to use Fire Insurance records at the Guildhall Library)

www.history.ac.uk/gh/sun.htm (How to access the online Sun Fire Office policy registers 1811–1835)

FREEMEN, GUILDS & LIVERY COMPANIES

Traditionally, Freemen had the right to elect the mayor, sheriff and aldermen of their town or city and to stand as Parliamentary representative. Until the 1800s normally one could only become a Freeman by one of three processes: namely through birth, through apprenticeship to another Freeman or by appointment. The position had other privileges, depending on which town, city or borough was concerned, mostly with regards to business or carrying out a trade. Guilds were associations of craftsmen and their records go back to medieval times – in London they were known as Livery Companies.

tinyurl.com/co58l6l (City of Derry Freemen)
tinyurl.com/cgx578h (London's freemen records on Ancestry.com)
www.findmypast.co.uk/search/other-records/freemen-of-ipswich (Ipswich Freemen)
www.batharchives.co.uk/family_history/civic_records.aspx (Bath Freemen + other records)
archivedatabases.cheshire.gov.uk/cms/lacfreemenofchester/home.aspx (Chester Freemen)
www.middle-ages.org.uk/medieval-london-guilds.htm (All about medieval Guilds)
www.exeter.gov.uk/index.aspx?articleid=3470 (Information about Freemen in Exeter)
www.muthergrumble.co.uk/issue05/mg0506.htm (Durham Freemen)
www.dur.ac.uk/library/asc/collection_information/cldload/?collno=43 (Durham Freemen)
www.guild-freemen-london.co.uk/help.php (Guild of Freemen of London)
en.wikipedia.org/wiki/Livery_Company (Wikipedia's links to all livery company pages)

GENEALOGICAL RESEARCH SERVICES

Many family history websites list or recommend professional family history researchers who will carry out genealogical research on your behalf. Regional libraries, archives and heritage centres are also useful in locating professional researchers, whose fees vary widely depending on their qualifications or geographical research areas.

www.agra.org.uk/ (Association of Genealogists and Researchers in Archives)
genealogypro.com/ (Find professional genealogists and specialised researchers here)

GENEALOGY CHAT ROOMS, FORUMS, LOOK-UPS, MESSAGE BOARDS & MAILING LISTS

These facilities allow family history researchers to make contact, chat, leave general enquiries, submit answers or place other material for anyone else to read. Chat Rooms and Message Boards allow individuals to talk online about a specific subject, in this case, genealogy. Many are linked to well-known genealogy sites and they are a useful way to exchange information, tips and experiences. When talking on Internet chat lines, users should be extremely careful about giving out their name and address or other personal details to contacts. Genealogical mailing lists are regular bulletins sent direct to your computer via e-mail. Most are free and are useful ways of keeping up with family history news and research, whilst Look-up sites provide a means of other people looking up information for you in family history records to which they have access. Here are a few samples, but you can search online for those dealing with your own interests.

www.rootschat.com/forum/ (Rootschat forums)
www.british-genealogy.com/forums/ (A selection of British genealogy forums)
tinyurl.com/cu9cbvo (Google's look-up page links)
www.parishregisteruklook-upexchange.co.uk/ (Parish register look-ups)
www.genlookups.com (Worldwide look-up volunteer exchange)
tinyurl.com/c5wv2pm (Google's Message Board page links)
tinyurl.com/o5xaesy (Helps you find a message board for any genealogical subject)
www.missing-you.net/Genealogy.php (Genealogy-based missing persons' message board to find details, photos, etc., of lost or dead relatives)
tinyurl.com/m3nmffe (A large selection of genealogy mailing lists, some of them quite specialized)

www.genuki.org.uk/indexes/MailingLists.html (A large selection of lists you can subscribe to)
freespace.virgin.net/genealogical.collections/cjmlists.htm (Explanation on using mailing lists with a selection of links to choose from)

GENEALOGY MAGAZINES

Family history magazines are a good source of tips and information for tracing family trees. Some include databases of information in either printed form or on free CDs given away with each issue. These are some of the major genealogy magazine websites.

www.family-tree.co.uk (*Family Tree Magazine* and *Practical Family History* – UK)
www.yourfamilytreemag.co.uk/ (*Your Family Tree Magazine* – UK)
www.aftc.com.au/ (*Australian Family Tree Connections* – Australia)
www.familytreemagazine.com/ (*Family Tree Magazine* – USA)
www.genealogymagazine.com/ (*Genealogy Magazine* – USA)

HOSPITALS & ASYLUMS

Hospital records are notoriously hard to get hold of and access may be restricted for reasons of confidentiality. You may need to carry out a number of searches in order to find the whereabouts of specific records. Below are examples of the types the diligent researcher could find. See also under **OCCUPATIONS** for medical, nursing and midwifery staff.

ALL RECORDS

www.nationalarchives.gov.uk/hospitalrecords/ (National Archives' database of hospital resources, including the old asylums)
www.medicalmuseums.org (London's hospital museums and archives, with links to websites)

HOSPITALS

tinyurl.com/bq27ex5 (Lots of historical UK hospital resources)
www.redcross.org.uk/Search?q=archive (British Red Cross Museum and Archives, with search facility to locate field hospitals, etc.)

homepage.ntlworld.com/jeffery.knaggs/I0109b.html (Patients and staff list of Casualty Ward, 86 East Street, Marylebone, London, in 1901)

homepage.ntlworld.com/jeffery.knaggs/I0259a.html (Patients and staff of City of London Lying-In Hospital, City Road, Finsbury, London, 1901)

homepage.ntlworld.com/jeffery.knaggs/I0612c.html (Patients and staff of Isolation Hospital, Mandora Barracks (Aldershot), Surrey, 1901)

homepage.ntlworld.com/jeffery.knaggs/I0971c.html (Patients and staff of Infirmary for West Sussex and East Hampshire, Broyle Road, Chichester, in 1901)

homepage.ntlworld.com/jeffery.knaggs/I1306b.html (Patients and staff at Hertford General Hospital, North Road, Hertford, in 1901)

ASYLUMS

tinyurl.com/cjm546t (Link to asylum records across the UK)

www.nationalarchives.gov.uk/records/research-guides/mental-health.htm (National Archives' guide to tracing asylum and health records)

www.berkshirerecordoffice.org.uk/albums/broadmoor/ (Broadmoor – Berkshire Record Office)

www.healtharchives.org/docs/Lunacy%20Codes.pdf (Researchers' guide to Medical Coding in Asylum Records in England and Wales)

www.familytreeforum.com/content.php/310-Hospital-Asylum-records (Forum and links)

www.findmypast.co.uk/search/other-records/prestwich-asylum-admissions (Search Prestwich asylum records)

www.institutions.org.uk/asylums/england/english_asylums.htm (Locate English asylums by county)

www.genuki.org.uk/search (Type 'asylums' into the search engine)

www.hertfordshire-genealogy.co.uk/data/topics/t070-long-stay-hospitals.htm (The 'long stay' hospitals of the St Albans' area)

www.hertfordshire-genealogy.co.uk/data/occupations/mad-houses.htm (Asylums in St Albans and Harpenden, with names and links)

www.hertfordshire-genealogy.co.uk/data/answers/answers-2003/ans-0305-taylor.htm (19th-century asylums near Watford)

yourarchives.nationalarchives.gov.uk/index.php?title=Broadmoor_Asylum (Tips on finding asylum records with links)

www.genuki.org.uk/big/eng/LIN/poorasylum.html (Page for researching Lincolnshire asylums)

genuki.cs.ncl.ac.uk/DEV/DevonIndexes/Asylum1880.html (Residents of Devon County Asylum 1880–1881)

LAND & PROPERTY

Inheritance and land ownership have always been strictly governed by law in Britain; consequently, records have been kept which stretch back to medieval times and beyond. Local tithe records are useful if your ancestor owned or resided on the land he worked; the Tithe Commutation Act of 1836 ensured the recording of the names of landowners and occupiers for most parishes throughout the country. Field names are also useful in pinpointing farmhouses and other buildings and in researching land sales and disputes. In the 12th century a procedure evolved for ending legal actions or disputes by an agreement known as final concords (or fines); by the 13th century the fine had become a popular way of conveying freehold property and the legal action involved was merely a device initiated by both parties to facilitate the transfer – the feet of fines were simply the portion of the document held by the court. See also **LAW & ORDER** and **MANORIAL RECORDS**.

ALL CATEGORIES

www.genuki.org.uk/search/ (Type the words 'land records' or 'land' separately, into this Genuki search engine to find over 5,000 local resources to choose from)

EXCHEQUER RECORDS

www.nationalarchives.gov.uk/records/looking-for-subject/taxation.htm (NA Records)
www.history.ac.uk/cmh/exchequer.html (Medieval Exchequer records guide)
www.londonancestor.com/leighs/crt-excheq.htm (Informative website with some good links)
catalog.hathitrust.org/Record/008645902 (Guide to Scottish Exchequer Records)

FEET OF FINES

www.british-history.ac.uk/search.asp?query1=%22feet+of+fines%22 (Links to Feet of Fines in UK with transcriptions)
www.medievalgenealogy.org.uk/fines/index.shtml (Explanation of the Feet of Fines legal procedure with links)
freespace.virgin.net/doug.thompson/BraoseWeb/family/feet2.html (Historic example and transcription of a Feet of Fine)

FIELD NAMES

tinyurl.com/c4u3xyv (Links to websites containing field name information throughout the UK)

tinyurl.com/dyscts2 (Google's field name resources)

www.fife.50megs.com/scottish-placenames-field-names.htm (Scottish field names)

www.burtonbradstock.org.uk/History/Old%20Maps/Field%20Names.htm (Example of a map showing field names)

REGISTRY OF DEEDS & RETURNS OF OWNERS OF LAND

tinyurl.com/d8oqrue (Land Registry & search)

www.wyjs.org.uk/archives-news.asp (West Yorkshire Registry of Deeds)

www.landregistry.gov.uk/professional/contacts/offices/responsible-areas2 (List of land registry offices by area)

www.genuki.org.uk/big/eng/YKS/Misc/Transcriptions/NRYland/index.html (List of North Yorkshire landowners 1871)

www.eylhs.org.uk/landed%20estates.pdf (Read 'East Yorkshire Landed Estates in the Nineteenth Century' online)

www.gov.im/registries/general/deeds_probate/ (Isle of Man Registry of Deeds site)

www.ros.gov.uk/professional/eservices/copy_deeds/index.html (Scottish Registry of Deeds)

www.nationalarchives.gov.uk/podcasts/irish-land-records.htm (Irish land records)

www.uk-genealogy.org.uk/datafiles/landtaxsearch.html (Search return of owners of land in 1873)

www.genuki.org.uk/search/ (Type 'return of owners' into this Genuki search engine to access over 900 resources dealing with land ownership)

www.genuki.org.uk/big/wal/GreatLandowners.html (Welsh landowners)

TITHES & ENCLOSURES

tinyurl.com/co88bek (Lots of links to tithe documentation in the UK and Ireland)

www.nationalarchives.gov.uk/records/research-guides/tithe-records.htm (National Archives guide to tithes and enclosures)

www.british-history.ac.uk/search.asp?query1=tithe (Records and resources from British History On-Line)

www.devon.gov.uk/tithe_records (Tithe records in Devon)

www.kentarchaeology.org.uk/Research/Maps/Maps%20intro.htm (Kent maps and tithe award schedules)

www.historic-maps.norfolk.gov.uk/emap/EMapExplorer.asp?PID=6&MTY=2&BID=0 (Norfolk tithe information and maps)
www.tracksintime.wyjs.org.uk (Leeds tithe map project)
www.worcestershire.gov.uk/cms/Search.aspx?terms=tithe%20maps (Worcestershire tithe and enclosure project)
maps.cheshire.gov.uk/tithemaps/ (Cheshire tithe maps online)**VALUATION RECORDS**
anws.llgc.org.uk/cgi-bin/anw/fulldesc_nofr?inst_id=28&coll_id=2238&expand= (Welsh valuation records)
tinyurl.com/clhmmlr (Guide to UK valuation records in The National Archives)
www.ancestralfindings.com/cd188.htm (Irish valuation records)
www.scotlandspeople.gov.uk/content/help/index.aspx?r=554&2080 (Valuation records in Scotland)

LAW & ORDER INCLUDING PUNISHMENTS, CRIMINALS, REFORM SCHOOLS, PRISONS

The wide range of historical documents now to be found on the Internet concerning all aspects of law and order make interesting reading. Here are just some of the thousands of resources, including those dealing with convicts who were sent to the colonies when transportation was seen both as a means of ridding Britain of its criminal classes and as a sure way to populate newly claimed lands. Contrary to popular opinion, transportation was not in itself a statutory punishment but was in most cases, at least initially, an option given to a prisoner who had been sentenced to death. Records of these and other criminals are constantly being gathered by individuals, commercial sites and family history societies and many are already available online.

ASSIZE AND QUARTER SESSION RECORDS

tinyurl.com/bwpym8e (Lots of quarter session links via Google)
www.british-history.ac.uk/catalogue.asp?gid=50 (British History Online website for searching Assize records)
yourarchives.nationalarchives.gov.uk/index.php?title=Research_Guide:_Assizes_-_Criminal_Trials (National Archives guide)
www.genuki.org.uk/search/ (Enter the words 'Quarter Sessions' into the search engine on this page to access nearly a thousand references countrywide)

BANKRUPTS

www.nationalarchives.gov.uk/records/looking-for-person/bankrupts.htm (Tracing bankrupts in The National Archives)

theoldentimes.com/bankrupts01021872uk.html (Scottish bankrupts)

CAPITAL PUNISHMENT

www.capitalpunishmentuk.org/1800.html (List of British public executions 1800–1827)

www.genuki.org.uk/big/eng/DUR/D_Executions.html (Executions at Durham, 1732–1909)

en.wikipedia.org/wiki/List_of_methods_of_capital_punishment (Historic list of methods of capital punishment)

www.capitalpunishmentuk.org/hangmen.html (English hangmen from 1850–1964)

www.capitalpunishmentuk.org/hanging1.html (British & Northern Ireland hangings 1735–1964)

www.from-ireland.net/irish-rebellion-1641-1642/ (Irish Hangings – 1641 rebellion)

CLOSE ROLLS, INQUISITIONS POST-MORTEM & PATENT ROLLS (LETTERS PATENT)

www.stradling.org.uk/docs/Cclr.htm (An explanation of the use of Close Rolls – concerning deeds, conveyances, etc., from the 13th century – for family history, with examples)

www.british-history.ac.uk/report.asp?compid=48091 (Page of explanation of Inquisitions Post-Mortem 13th century to 17th century – enquiries made after the death of a Crown landholder – with additional pages containing transcripts of early IPMs)

sdrc.lib.uiowa.edu/patentrolls/search.html (Browse or search British Patent Rolls – or Letters Patent – from 1216–1452; concerned the granting of rights and privileges)

COURT OF CHANCERY

tinyurl.com/dyjtw7c (Lots of Chancery record links from Genuki)

www.ancestry.co.uk/search/db.aspx?dbid=7919 (Search Chancery records 1386–1558; subscription site)

www.nas.gov.uk/guides/chancery.asp (Guide to Scottish Chancery records)

COURT OF KING'S BENCH

www.british-history.ac.uk/search.asp?query1=%22king%27s+bench%22 (Links to pages concerning King's Bench records, 12th to 19th centuries, which settled disputes when Crown property was involved)

COURT OF REQUESTS

www.nationalarchives.gov.uk/records/research-guides/court-of-requests.htm (National Archives Courts of Requests page)
en.wikipedia.org/wiki/Court_of_Requests (Wikipedia's explains the Court of Requests system)
www.victorianlondon.org/legal/requests.htm (London Court of Requests)

COURT OF STAR CHAMBER

www.british-history.ac.uk/report.asp?compid=48094 (Explanation of the court proceedings of the Star Chamber, with links)

COURT OF WARDS & LIVERIES

tinyurl.com/cbtpcot (National Archives guide)
www.aim25.ac.uk/cgi-bin/search2?coll_id=3205&inst_id=14 (Records of the Court of Wards and Liveries at the Senate House Library, London and access details)

COURT RECORDS & FINES (GENERAL)

tinyurl.com/d88gley (Misc. UK court record links)
www.oldbaileyonline.org/ (Search London's Old Bailey court records)
tinyurl.com/cyqtnkv (Records in the Corporation of London Record Office)
www.scotlandspeople.gov.uk/content/help/index.aspx?r=551&565 (About the Scottish court system with links to records useful to family historians)
www.wirksworth.org.uk/CRIME.htm (Crime records in Derbyshire 1770–1828)
www.nas.gov.uk/guides/sheriffCourt.asp (Scottish Sheriff Court records)
www.victorianlondon.org/legal/dickens-lawcourts.htm (Detailed study of Victorian London courts)

CRIMINALS

www.nationalarchives.gov.uk/documentsonline/prison.asp (Online Victorian prisoners' photographs at The National Archives)

pinterest.com/twmuseums/criminal-faces-1871-1873/ ('Mugshots' of Tyne and Wear criminals)

www.genuki.org.uk/search/ (Enter the word 'crime' or 'criminal')

www.exclassics.com/newgate/ngintro.htm (Links to lists of criminals under various criminal headings)

freespace.virgin.net/genealogical.collections/NaughtyFolk.htm (Some Wiltshire criminal records 1864–1855)

www.genuki.org.uk/big/wal/WelshMurders.html (Welsh murders 1770–1918)

Prisoners at Coldbath Fields House of Correction, Clerkenwell, London.
© *2014 Colin Waters Collection*

Law & Order Including Punishments, Criminals, Reform Schools, Prisons

EYRES

www.british-history.ac.uk/subject.asp?subject=1&gid=49 (Records of Eyres and other administrative/legal history)
www.british-history.ac.uk/search.asp?query1=london+eyre (Links to records and information)

OUTLAWS & HIGHWAYMEN

tinyurl.com/bp6rhj8 (Google's links to resources about highwaymen)
www.outlawsandhighwaymen.com/links.htm (Links to outlaw and highwaymen resources)
www.british-history.ac.uk/search.asp?query1=HIGHWAYMAN (Historic documents and references regarding highwaymen)

PARDONS & CLEMENCY PLEAS

tinyurl.com/d87kae6 (Guide to licences, pardons and clemency plea files in The National Archives)

PRISONS, CONVICTS AND TRANSPORTATION

tinyurl.com/cnhsga7 (Prisoner and gaol links from GENUKI)
www.nationalarchives.gov.uk/documentsonline/prison.asp (Online Victorian prisoners' photographs at The National Archives)
www.genuki.org.uk/search/ (Enter the words 'prisoners' and 'gaol' into this search engine to access over 800 resources regarding UK and Irish prisoners)
en.wikipedia.org/wiki/List_of_prisons_in_the_United_Kingdom (List of historical prisons)
www.exclassics.com/newgate/ngintro.htm (The Newgate Calendar, with lists of criminals under various headings)
www.convictcentral.com/ (Large database specifically aimed at researching transported convict ancestors)
members.pcug.org.au/~ppmay/convicts.htm (Search for Irish convicts transported to New South Wales)
members.pcug.org.au/~ppmay/austlinks.htm (Links to sites in Australia that specialise in convict research)
home.vicnet.net.au/%7Edcginc/frames.htm#top (Descendants of convicts' website with 'Members Convict' link to lists of men and women sent to Australia)

homepages.ihug.co.nz/~tonyf/parkhurstboys/convicts4.html (Parkhurst prisoners sent to New Zealand)

www.yorkcastleprison.org.uk/family-history/condemned (Search York Castle prison inmates online)

PUNISHMENTS

tinyurl.com/cpayprd (Lots of links from Google, including historical, military, prison, factory and local punishments)

history.powys.org.uk/history/common/crimenu.html (A look at how offenders were punished in Wales)

www.llgc.org.uk/sesiwn_fawr/index_s.htm (Crime and punishment database search)

score.rims.k12.ca.us/score_lessons/colonial_court/html/colonial.html (Punishments of servants in the American colonies)

REFORM SCHOOLS, INDUSTRIAL SCHOOLS & BORSTALS

yourarchives.nationalarchives.gov.uk/index.php?title=Industrial_and_Reformatory_Schools (National Archive records)

www.institutions.org.uk/reformatories/index.html (Reformatories and Industrial Schools web page)

homepage.ntlworld.com/jeffery.knaggs/I2386a.html (List of those at the Convent of the Good Shepherd Reformatory School for Girls, Bristol, 1901)

STATUTE & COMMON LAW

www.nationalarchives.gov.uk/records/looking-for-person/civil-litigant.htm (How to find litigation records)

www.nationalarchives.gov.uk/records/research-guides/crime-and-law.htm (National Archives page)

www.statutelaw.gov.uk/Home.aspx (UK Statute Law Database – search here for any law throughout history by name, date or type)

www.medievalgenealogy.org.uk/guide/leg.shtml (Guide to miscellaneous branches of Common Law with links)

WITCH TRIALS

www.witchtrials.co.uk/ (Essex witch trials)

tinyurl.com/c3j6bjb (Witch trials at North Berwick)
www.genuki.org.uk/search/ (Type the word 'witch' into this Genuki search engine to access over 100 references and sources regarding witches in the UK and Ireland)
www.british-history.ac.uk/search.asp?query1=witchcraft (Historic references to witches, witchcraft trials and official documents)
www.hulford.co.uk/essex.html (Essex witchcraft trials with associated information – search facility)
www.hulford.co.uk/trials.html (English witch trials with search)
www.lowestoftwitches.com/ (Lowestoft witch trial website)
www.pendlewitches.co.uk/ (All about the Pendle, Lancashire witches)

LOCAL HISTORY SOCIETIES & GROUPS

Local history and family history often go hand in hand and for those who want to find out more about the way an ancestor lived, joining a local history society is often the quickest way to meet like-minded and knowledgeable individuals.

tinyurl.com/c7sdkna (Genuki's list of local history societies)
www.local-history.co.uk/Groups/ (Lists of national and regional local history societies)
www.balh.co.uk/index.php (Website of the British Association for Local History)

MANORIAL RECORDS

Manorial records – which may be as recent as the early 20th century in some areas – include such documents as court rolls, surveys, maps, terriers, and all other documents relating to the boundaries, franchises, wastes, customs or courts of a manor. Some may still be found locally but the best central source for British records is The National Archives.

tinyurl.com/d9gt9t8 (Manorial records and documents from Genuki)
www.nationalarchives.gov.uk/mdr/ (The National Archives Manorial Documents Register site)
www.isle-of-man.com/manxnotebook/fulltext/manroll/ (Manorial rolls of Isle of Man translated from Latin)
www.genuki.org.uk/big/#Manors (Miscellaneous manorial links plus other records)

MAPS & GAZETTEERS

Using old maps and gazetteers is an important aid for anyone researching their family tree, whether it is for locating towns and villages, finding the site of an ancestral home or tracking down an old inn, cemetery or street name. Because of the constant changes to town and county boundaries and place-names, not to mention the demolition of whole streets of buildings and the erection of others on former country fields and waste sites, maps are often essential in understanding the past and its relationship to present times.

GENERAL MAP RESOURCES

www.britainfromabove.org.uk/ (Historic pictures of places in Britain taken from the air)
tinyurl.com/d3thr7h (An excellent source of viewable online maps)
geo.nls.uk/partners/wilbourn/ (Scottish maps)
www.visionofbritain.org.uk/maps/ (Vision of Britain map site)
freepages.genealogy.rootsweb.ancestry.com/~genmaps/ (Genmaps site)
www.genuki.org.uk/big/eng/Maps.html (Links to old map resources throughout Britain)
www.old-maps.co.uk/ (Commercial site – look for and purchase old maps)
www.visionofbritain.org.uk/maps/index.jsp (British map resource 1801–2001)
www.antique-maps-online.co.uk/ (Online antique maps)
www.hipkiss.org/data/links.html (Links to old maps and charts)
www.leitrim-roscommon.com/heraldry/heraldry.html (Website with an interesting map of Ireland as it was in medieval times, c1300)

COUNTY, LOCAL & REGIONAL MAPS

www.historiccoventry.co.uk/covmaps/allmaps.php (Coventry maps & plans from early times)
booth.lse.ac.uk/ (Booths poverty maps of London)
www.newforest.hampshire.org.uk/historic_maps/maps_intro.html (Historic maps of the New Forest)
www.historic-maps.norfolk.gov.uk/mapimageviewer/ (Historic Norfolk maps)
www.birmingham.gov.uk/historicalmaps (Old maps of Birmingham)
www.edinphoto.org.uk/0_maps/0_maps_thumbnails.htm (Edinburgh historic maps)
www.alangodfreymaps.co.uk/yorkshire.htm (Old Yorkshire maps)
www.chesterwalls.info/gallery/oldmaps/index.html (Old maps and views from the air – Chester)

www.genuki.org.uk/big/Britain.html (Counties of England, Wales and Scotland prior to the 1974 Boundary Changes)
www.genuki.org.uk/search/ (Type 'parish map' into the search engine on this page to find thousands of links and references to parish maps throughout the UK and Ireland)
www.gazetteer.co.uk/gazmap1.htm (Map showing old counties of Britain)
www.gazetteer.co.uk/gazmap2.htm (Map of modern British county and unitary administrative authorities)
users.bathspa.ac.uk/greenwood/lplaces.html (Online maps of old London)
www.geog.port.ac.uk/webmap/hantsmap/hantsmap/hantsmap.htm (Old Hampshire maps)
www.genuki.org.uk/big/sct/sct_cmap.html (County map of Scotland)

FIELD MAPS

www.shropshire.gov.uk/archives.nsf/open/9FEBD76063D9E0C5802574E600324C78 (Shropshire field maps)
www.archelou.co.uk/ercall_maps/Field_maps_index.htm (Ercall Magna field maps)
www.blisworth.org.uk/images/Farming/Fields/field_maps.htm (Blisworth, Northants. field maps)
www.burtonbradstock.org.uk/History/Old%20Maps/Field%20Names.htm (Example of a map showing field names)

ORDNANCE SURVEY MAPS

www.ordnancesurvey.co.uk/oswebsite/ (Website of the Ordnance Survey)
www.alangodfreymaps.co.uk/ (Find reprints of old UK Ordnance Survey maps)
www.british-history.ac.uk/map.asp (Search for old Ordnance Survey maps using online gazetteer search facility)

SATELLITE MAPS

www.brighthub.com/internet/google/articles/61335.aspx (Alternatives to Google Earth)
earth.google.com/ (Download 'Google Earth' free and use satellite images to locate countries, places and street locations or even to zoom in on your own house)
www.flashearth.com/ (Satellite and aerial images)
www.metoffice.gov.uk/weather/satellite/ (Weather satellite images)

SEA AREAS

www.metoffice.gov.uk/weather/marine/guide/shipping/key.html (British sea areas mentioned in weather forecasts with weather details)

GAZETTEERS, PLACE & STREETFINDERS

www.theaa.com/maps/index.jsp (Search for any place using AA facilities)
www.genuki.org.uk/big/Gazetteers.html (Gazetteers from Genuki)
www.gazetteer.co.uk/section1.htm (Gazetteer of over 50,000 British place-names)
www.geo.ed.ac.uk/scotgaz/ (Scottish gazetteer)
www.history.ac.uk/cmh/gaz/gazweb2.html (Gazetteer of Markets and Fairs in England and Wales up to 1516)
www.british-history.ac.uk/source.asp?pubid=8 (Historical Gazetteer of London before the Great Fire 1666)
intarch.ac.uk/journal/issue3/snyder_index.html (Gazetteer of sub-Roman Britain)
www.fallingrain.com/world/EI/ (Irish gazetteer)
homepage.ntlworld.com/geogdata/ngw/home.htm (National Gazetteer of Wales)
maps.yahoo.com/ (Yahoo maps and direction finder)
www.streetmap.co.uk (Modern street map finder)
maps.google.co.uk/ (Google maps – find places and streets, as well as towns)

MEDIEVAL GENEALOGY

Modern technology means that more and more people are able to trace their family trees back to medieval times. Below is a sample of some of the websites that may assist in your search.

www.medievalsources.co.uk/ (Medieval sources online)
www.medievalgenealogy.org.uk/ (A general guide to families and resources for this period)
fmg.ac/ (Foundation for Medieval Genealogy for promoting and studying this period)
freepages.genealogy.rootsweb.com/~tapperofamily/abbrev.html (List of abbreviations used in medieval genealogy)
www.castles.me.uk/medieval-occupations.htm (Occupations in medieval times)
www.medievalgenealogy.org.uk/sources/brasses1.shtml (Links to monumental brasses on the Internet)
www.domesdaybook.co.uk/ (Online Domesday Book with search facility)
www.middle-ages.org.uk/medieval-london-guilds.htm (All about medieval guilds)
www.medievalgenealogy.org.uk/cal/medcal.shtml (A medieval calendar)

NEWSPAPER & MAGAZINE RESOURCES

Most newspapers hold archives going back to their first edition, though not all are available to the public. Access to a growing number is now available via the Internet, both as free and paid services. The digital index to The Times may be available through your local library or record office. The following is just a small selection; others can be obtained by typing the newspaper or periodical's name into a search engine.

www.britishnewspaperarchive.co.uk/ (British Newspaper Archives – Pay to view)

tinyurl.com/bowyre4 (Lots of online resources from national and regional newspaper sources)

www.ambaile.org/en/newspapers/index.jsp (Searchable Scottish newspaper archives) – Worldwide newspaper links)

tinyurl.com/c9jxnzw (Australian newspapers, periodicals and more!)

paperspast.natlib.govt.nz/cgi-bin/paperspast (Historic New Zealand newspapers)

guides.library.ubc.ca/newspapers (Researching Canadian newspapers)

www.uk-family-history.com/TheTimes.html (*Times* Digital Archives)

www.gazettes-online.co.uk (Search the archives of the London, Edinburgh & Belfast gazettes)

www.genuki.org.uk/search/ (Enter 'newspapers' in the search field to access over 2,000 separate old newspaper resources countrywide)

www.bodley.ox.ac.uk/ilej/ (Free searchable library of early journals)

www.thepaperboy.com/ (One of the world's leading sites for finding newspapers around the world)

tinyurl.com/cufms3x (British Library newspaper collection online)

archive.scotsman.com/ (The *Scotsman* digital archive)

www.swansea.gov.uk/index.cfm?articleid=5673 (Search the index of the first Welsh, English-language newspaper 1804–1930)

www.old-liverpool.co.uk/ (A collection of items from Liverpool newspapers including Births, Marriages and Deaths)

http://guardian.chadwyck.co.uk/password (Archives of the *Guardian* and the *Observer*)

www.genuki.org.uk/big/eng/YKS/Misc/Transcriptions/NRY/MaltonMessenger 1856BDM.html (Transcriptions of Births, Marriages and Deaths from the Yorkshire *Malton Messenger* in 1856)

www.origins.org.uk/genuki/NFK/norfolk/newspapers/extracts.shtml (Transcribed extracts from Norfolk newspapers) turnertree.net/newspaper.html (1913 Devon newspaper extracts, including births, marriages and deaths)

oldenglishnewspapers.com/ (Various old newspaper extracts)

http://en.wikipedia.org/wiki/Wikipedia:List_of_online_newspaper_archives (Wikipedia list of online newspaper archives worldwide)

www.bl.uk / (British Library site with search facility)

NOBILITY & ARISTOCRACY

If you think or know that you are descended from aristocratic or even royal stock, then there is a possibility that you may be able to trace your lineage further back than most. Here are a few sites that could assist you in your researches. See also under **COATS OF ARMS**.

www.scotlandroyalty.org/peerage.html (Peerage & Nobility of the British Isles)

familysearch.org/learn/wiki/en/England_Nobility#Sources (Researching English nobility)

archive.org/stream/biographicalpee00unkngoog#page/n8/mode/2up (read The Biological Peerage of Ireland online)

www.almanachdegotha.org/ (Royalty – Almanach de Saxe Gotha)

fmg.ac/Projects/MedLands/BURGUNDY%20Kingdom.htm (Burgundy nobility)

fmg.ac/Project s/MedLands/NORMAN%20NOBILITY.htm (Medieval Norman nobility)

thepeerage.com/ (Genealogical matters relating to the peerage of Britain including a discussion group)

www.hereditarytitles.com / (Site dedicated to hereditary titles of the British Empire)

www.burkespeerage.com (Burke's Peerage site)

OCCUPATIONS

Our family history research is undeniably enhanced by finding out about the occupations of our forebears. Knowing about their trades, what they did and where they worked can add understanding and interest to our knowledge of their past. There are now lots of lists, large and small, on the Internet that concentrate on individual trades and occupations, often with valuable supplementary information. For older and more obscure occupations see the Countryside Books ebook – *A Dictionary of Old Trades, Titles and Occupations*. See also **DIRECTORIES**.

ALL OCCUPATIONS

www.genuki.org.uk/search/ (Type 'occupations' to search lots of internet resources dealing with various trades and jobs; also search for individual occupations)
rmhh.co.uk/occup/ (Select occupations by starting letter)
www.wcml.org.uk/ (The Working Class Movement Library with links and resources)
www.genuki.org.uk/big/Occupations.html (Selection of Genuki occupational links)
www.scotsfamily.com/occupations.htm (Scottish occupations)
www.usgenweb.org/research/occupations.shtml (US site listing occupations)
www.castles.me.uk/medieval-occupations.htm (Medieval occupations)
tinyurl.com/c46mnvc (Trade records for family historians by category with links to other records)
www.movinghere.org.uk/galleries/roots/caribbean/occupations/occupations.htm (Information with links on recruitment of Caribbean men to UK civil service posts, Merchant Navy, military, etc.)
http://german.about.com/library/blgenevoc_berufe.htm (German occupations)
http://www.reocities.com/heartland/pointe/8783/italjobs.html (Translation of Italian occupations)
www.historicaldirectories.org (Trades directories for the UK. Search by location, decade or keyword)

AGRICULTURE

www.reading.ac.uk/Instits/imcopy/rural/hist.html (Rural history centre)
tinyurl.com/cmwzgsh (Thousands of genealogy links to resources that mention farmers)
www.genuki.org.uk/search/ (Search here for UK and Ireland agricultural records using the term most appropriate, e.g. 'drovers' or 'farmers')
www.bahs.org.uk/ (Website of the British Agricultural History Society)
www.genuki.org.uk/big/wal/WelshDrovers.html (Info on Welsh cattle drovers)
www.reading.ac.uk/merl/ (Museum of English Rural Life)

APPRENTICESHIPS & INDENTURES

tinyurl.com/5r8rane (National Archive guide to researching apprentices)
www.genuki.org.uk/search/ (Type the word 'apprentice' into this search engine to access over 1,000 apprenticeship and indenture sources throughout Britain and Ireland)
www.berksfhs.org.uk/journal/Dec2002/ApprenticeshipDocuments.htm (Berkshire apprenticeship records)

genuki.cs.ncl.ac.uk/DEV/Jacobstowe/JacobstoweSettlements.html (Jacobstowe, Devon, apprenticeships & settlements)
www.nationalarchives.gov.uk/podcasts/apprenticeship-records.htm (Apprenticeship records at The National Archives)
www.mariners-l.co.uk/UKApprentices.html (Advice on tracing Navy apprentices)

ARTISTS

tinyurl.com/c3bps3v (Biographies of portrait miniature artists)
myweb.tiscali.co.uk/speel/london/londart.htm (Links to biographies of Victorian artists)
www.victorianweb.org/painting/paintingov.html (Information on Victorian painters)
witcombe.sbc.edu/ARTHLinks.html (General art history resource site)

BANKERS

www.victorianlondon.org/finance/listofbanks.htm (A list of banks in Victorian London)
victorianresearch.org/bankmergers.txt (List of minor banks that merged)
www.scotbanks.org.uk/banking_history.php (Scottish banking history)
www.danbyrnes.com.au/merchants/ (Chronologically lists merchants, bankers and related history from earliest times to 2002)
http://www.bankofengland.co.uk/archive/Pages/default.aspx (Bank of England archives)

BLACKSMITHS

www.hunimex.com/warwick/smiths_indx.html (Warwickshire blacksmiths)
blacksmiths.mygenwebs.com/bristol-1.php (Bristol blacksmiths)
www.blacksmithscompany.org.uk/Pages/History/History_Incorporation.htm (Website of the Worshipful Company of Blacksmiths)

BOILERMAKERS

www.nationalarchives.gov.uk/A2A/records.aspx?cat=050-dx116&cid=0#0 (United Society of Boilermakers' records)
blacksmiths.mygenwebs.com/boilers-1.php (Boilermakers' database)
www.wcml.org.uk/contents/working-lives/boilermakers/ (Sources for boilermakers' records)

BONNET MAKERS

www.rootschat.com/forum/index.php/topic,561499.0.html (Edinburgh bonnet makers)
www.hatsuk.com/hatsuk/hatsukhtml/directory/directoryintro.htm (Misc. hat-makers' links)
www.llangynfelyn.org/dogfennau/hetwyr_saesneg.html (Welsh bonnet and hat makers)
www.ninetradesofdundee.co.uk/bonnet_makers.html (Dundee bonnet makers)
tinyurl.com/lzyjlx2 (About Glasgow bonnet makers)

BOOK TRADE

www.bbti.bham.ac.uk/ (An index of names and brief biographical and trade details of those in England and Wales trading by 1851, with link to a similar Scottish index)

BREWERS & DISTILLERS

tinyurl.com/cwrl948 (Google's brewery links)
tinyurl.com/cvnvckg (Google's distillery links)
www.breweryhistory.com/links.htm (Brewery history society links)
www.mkheritage.co.uk/nphs/docs/museum/brewerybottles.html (Breweries in Newport Pagnell)
www.midlandspubs.co.uk/ (Midland pubs and breweries)
http://www.guinness-storehouse.com/en/Archive.aspx (How to access the Guinness Archives)

BRICKMAKERS

tinyurl.com/bqwmzu6 (Browse Google's list of local brickworks)
www.brickdirectory.co.uk/ (The brickmakers' index)
tinyurl.com/k2qdyc8 (Hertfordshire brickmakers 1851)
www.colepotteries.co.uk/lewisham-earthworks.htm (Lewisham brickmakers. Also potters)
tinyurl.com/cd9xtsj (Brickmakers of Leverstock Green)

BRUSHMAKERS

www.wcml.org.uk/contents/trade-unions/brushmakers/ (Union records)
tinyurl.com/cqenf4j (Countrywide links to documents mentioning individual brushmakers)
www.brushmakers.com/ (Home page for the Society of Brushmakers' Descendants)

BUTCHERS

tinyurl.com/d4josqv (Countrywide links to documents mentioning individual butchers)
history.foote-family.com/butchers/ (History of Guernsey butchers)
www.butchershall.com/ (Worshipful Company of Butchers site)
www.yorkbutchersgild.com/pages/history.html (York Company of Butchers)

CANALS & WATERWAYS

en.wikipedia.org/wiki/List_of_waterway_societies_in_the_United_Kingdom (List of Waterway Societies)
www.virtualwaterways.co.uk/home.html (National Waterways Archive with links to other similar archives)
www.bargemen.co.uk/ (Website of 'The Barge Men' with links to names, etc.)
freespace.virgin.net/anglers.rest/Canalpeople.htm (Forum for those researching family trees amongst those who lived and worked on canals and waterways)
www.canaljunction.com/canal/heritage.htm (Website dedicated to the heritage of the canals of Britain)
www.canalmuseum.org.uk/collection/family-history.htm (Family history tips and links for searching for canal and waterway workers)
www.genuki.org.uk/big/eng/STS/Names/WolvCanal.html (Baptisms and marriages of Wolverhampton canal people)
www.hertfordshire-genealogy.co.uk/data/census/census1881-bargebuilders.htm (A list of Hertfordshire barge builders in 1881)
www.msurman.freeserve.co.uk/www/pages/Glos%20Strays.htm (Gloucester 'strays' on boats in 1841 census)
www.jim-shead.com/waterways/Engindex.html (Index of waterway engineers and surveyors)
www.jim-shead.com/waterways/Peopleindex.html (Index of waterway people)
www.virtualwaterways.co.uk/home.html (Virtual Waterways Archive Catalogue)
www.rchs.org.uk/trial/gwpf.php?wpage=home (Website of the Railway and Canal Historical Society)

CHARTERED ACCOUNTANTS

www.familytreeconnection.com/resources/ftc366.html (Search the membership list of the Institute of Chartered Accountants in Ireland 1916)
www.icaew.co.uk/library/index.cfm?AUB=TB2I_27022 (Institute of Chartered Accountants in England and Wales' library and information service)

CHEMISTS & ALCHEMISTS

www.unilever.com/aboutus/ourhistory/unilever_archives/ (Archives of Unilever & associated companies)
www.open.ac.uk/ou5/Arts/chemists/ (Biographical database of the British Chemical Community, 1880–1970)

CIRCUS & FAIRGROUND WORKERS

circusfolk.freeservers.com/ (Circus-folk site with genealogy links)
www.shef.ac.uk/nfa/ (Website of the National Fairground Archive)
www.circushistory.org/ (Website of the Circus Historical Society)
members.shaw.ca/pauline777/TravellersUK.html (Links and lists relating to showmen, circus and fairground travellers)
boards.ancestry.co.uk/topics.occupations.circus/mb.ashx (Circus genealogy discussion & message board)
www.rootschat.com/forum/index.php/topic,362110.msg2350545.html (Traveller, Circus, Fairground and Gypsy website links)

CLERGYMEN & MISSIONARIES

archives.lambethpalacelibrary.org.uk/calmview/ (Lambeth Palace Database of Manuscripts and Archives)
www.history.ac.uk/gh/clergy.htm (Guildhall Library Manuscripts Section Sources for tracing clergy and lay persons)
www.theclergydatabase.org.uk/ (Database whose objective is to document the careers of all C of E clergymen 1540–1835)
www.british-history.ac.uk/search.asp?query1=clergy (Historical lists and documents relating to the clergy)
http://divdl.library.yale.edu/missionperiodicals/ (Missionary periodicals database)
www.vt-fcgs.org/catholic.html (US and Canadian Roman Catholic missionaries)
www-sul.stanford.edu/africa/history/missionarymicroforms.html (Guide to sources for African missionaries)
www.wheaton.edu/bgc/archives/archhp1.html (Billy Graham Centre archives with links)
www.crockford.org.uk/ (Crockford's Clerical Directory web page)
www.mundus.ac.uk/ (Gateway to missionary collections in the UK)
webarchive.cms-uk.org/library.htm (Website of the Church Mission Society with details of how to access records)

CLOCK & WATCH MAKERS

www.bhi.co.uk/aHJ/obits1.html (British Horological Institute list of obituaries)
www.clockmakers.org (Worshipful Company of Clockmakers site)

COACHMEN & CARRIERS

archive.org/stream/oldcoachingdays00bradgoog#page/n4/mode/2up (Read *Old Coaching Days in Yorkshire* online – lots of names)
www.genuki.org.uk/search/ (Type the words 'coaches', 'coachman' and 'carrier' separately into this search engine to get hundreds of links to trade directories)
www.british-history.ac.uk/report.asp?compid=43923 (Historic coachman resources)

COASTGUARDS & CUSTOMS OFFICERS

www.coastguardsofyesteryear.org/news.php (Irish Coastguards)
www.trinityhouse.co.uk/corporation/genealogy.html (Trinity House genealogy links)
www.mcga.gov.uk/c4mca/mcga07-home (Maritime & Coastguard Agency search page – search for 'Genealogy')
www.hillsd.freeserve.co.uk/marhist/shoreidx.htm (Smuggling site with access to names, including customs officers, places and ships)
www.nationalarchives.gov.uk/records/looking-for-person/coastguard.htm (Coastguards information from The National Archives)
www.genuki.org.uk/big/Coastguards/index.html (A list of British Coastguards 1841–1901)
www.mariners-l.co.uk/UKCustoms.html (Details of official documents available for researching Customs staff)

COBBLERS, BOOT & SHOEMAKERS

www.genuki.org.uk/search/ (Type the words 'shoemaker', 'cobbler' or 'cordwainer' into the search engine)
www.genuki.org.uk/big/eng/YKS/Misc/Trades/Boot_shoe_makers_of_Yorkshire2.txt (List of Yorkshire boot and shoe makers)
www.genuki.org.uk/big/eng/YKS/Misc/Trades/Boot_shoe_makers_of_Yorkshire.txt (More Yorkshire boot & shoemakers)
www.british-history.ac.uk/report.aspx?compid=48166 (Records of the Cardiff Cordwainers and Glovers)
tinyurl.com/bqxmu8d (Some Nottingham shoe and boot makers)

CUTLERS

www.cutlerslondon.co.uk/ (Worshipful Company of Cutlers website)
www.cutlers-hallamshire.org.uk/html/the-cutlers-hall/ (Cutlers Hall website)
www.sheffieldindexers.com/MasterCutlersMayorsIndex.html (List of Master Cutlers 1624–1925)

DENTISTS

www.genesreunited.co.uk/boards/board/tips_board/thread/853953 (Genealogy chat page)
www.genealogyforum.co.uk/forum/viewtopic.php?f=33&t=15570 (Family Tree Forum)
www.bda.org/museum/enquiries/was-ancestor-dentist.aspx (British Dental Association website)

DIVERS

www.olddivers.co.uk/Database.htm (Old Divers database)
www.thehds.com/ (Find out how to search the Historical Diving Society's database of divers and associated trades)

DOCTORS, PHYSICIANS & MEDICAL SUBJECTS

tinyurl.com/co54szj (Welcome Library Doctors resources)
www.medicalmuseums.org/ (London museums of health and medicine)
www.history.ac.uk/gh/apoths.htm (Guildhall records of apothecaries, surgeons, physicians and medical practitioners, including barber-surgeons)
www.ums.ac.uk/archives.html (Ulster Medical Science Archives website)
histsciences.univ-paris1.fr/databases/cpl/ (Irregular Practitioners 1550–1640 database and book)
www.familyrelatives.com/navigate/navigate_detail.php?id=4 (Search for doctors, dentists and midwives in medical registers)

DYERS

www.british-history.ac.uk/report.aspx?compid=59925 (Historical records)
www.dyerscompany.co.uk/ (Worshipful Company of Dyers website)

EAST INDIA COMPANY

www.eicships.info/ (Information about East India Company ships)
www.londonlives.org/static/AHDSEIC.jsp (British East India Company: Salaries paid to 'Clerks', 1760–1820)
tinyurl.com/ch8b52q (About East India Company records, 1752–1772)
www.aigs.org.au/britind.htm (Information and links about the East India Company)

ENGINEERING AND TECHNOLOGY

tinyurl.com/c3apqbq (How to research the records of the Amalgamated Engineering Union)
tinyurl.com/d6sy9ow (About the records of the Heating and Domestic Engineers' Union and predecessors 1911–1967)
search.theiet.org/iet/search?action=IETSearch&q=archives (Archive collection of material held to promote and preserve the history of engineering and technology)
www.ice.org.uk/topics/historicalengineering/Archives (Institute of Civil Engineers' heritage archives)
www.cornucopia.org.uk/html/search/verb/GetRecord/6735 (Clickable links to the Institute of Civil Engineers' library)

FIREMEN

archiveshub.ac.uk/features/firefighters.shtml (Archives Hub firefighters page)
www.firepolicemuseum.org.uk/ (Fire & Police Museum)
www.museumsgalleriesscotland.org.uk/member/Museum-of-Fire (Museum of Fire)
www.london-fire.gov.uk/OurHistory.asp (Research resource for the London Fire Service)
www.wafersmuseum.org.uk/ (Welsh Museum of Fire)
www.genuki.org.uk/search/ (Enter 'fireman' and 'firemen' into this Genuki search engine to find hundreds of individual sources concerning firemen)
www.fireservice.co.uk/history (History research resources for the Fire Service)

FISHERMEN & WHALERS

www.genuki.org.uk/search/ (Search the Genuki archives using the words 'fisherman' or 'fishing' to obtain hundreds of genealogical resources throughout the UK and Ireland)
www.mariners-l.co.uk/UKFishermen.html (The mariners mailing list – tracing fishermen in British waters)
www.mariners-l.co.uk/Grimsbyfishermendeaths.html (Board of Trade list of drowned mariners reported at Grimsby 1878–1882)

www.mariners-l.co.uk/Hullfishermendeaths.html (Hull fishermen who died at sea 1878–1882)

www.edinphoto.org.uk/0_a_l/0_around_edinburgh_-_newhaven.htm (Old photographs relating to fishermen and fishing)

www.explorenorth.com/whalers/ (Whalers Heritage Project for researching whaling ancestors)

explorenorth.com/whalers/ships-whitby.html (List of whale boats sailing from Whitby 1753–1837)

explorenorth.com/whalers/whalers.htm (Whalers Index from the Whalers Heritage Project)

explorenorth.com/whalers/crew-prospect.html (Crew list of the whaling ship *Prospect*, of Whitby 1788)

explorenorth.com/whalers/crew-volunteer.html (Crew lists of the Whaling ship *Volunteer*, 1772 and 1815)

A sturgeon caught off Glasson Dock, displayed outside Nicholsons Boatyard, Lancashire.

FLESHERS

tinyurl.com/ckm8osv (List of members of the Flesher Craft, 1859)
www.ninetradesofdundee.co.uk/fleshers.html (Dundee fleshers)

GAS WORKERS

www.johnhearfield.com/Gas/Gas_strike.htm (All about the 1890 Leeds gas-workers dispute)
www.gasarchive.org/ (National Gas Archive website)
www.spartacus.schoolnet.co.uk/TUgas.htm (Website of the National Union of Gasworkers)

GLOVERS

www.thegloverscompany.org/ (Worshipful Company of Glovers of London website)
oxoniensia.org/vol%203/Schulz.doc (All about the Woodstock glove makers)
www.british-history.ac.uk/report.aspx?compid=48166 (Records of the Cardiff Cordwainers and Glovers)

GUNMAKERS & ALLIED TRADES

www.gunmakers.org.uk/ (Worshipful Company of Gunmakers site)
www.genuki.org.uk/big/Gunmakers.html (Details of Index of over 9,000 names)
http://www.internetgunclub.com/Modules/Login.aspx (Search the Internet Gun Club's database of gunmakers – Registration required)

GYPSY, ROMANY & TRAVELLERS RECORDS

archiveshub.ac.uk/features/jun06.shtml (Lots of Romany links)
romanygenes.webeden.co.uk/ (Romany Genes website)
www.rtfhs.org.uk/ (Site dedicated to the family history of travelling communities, their employment, history, culture and background)
romanygenes2.webeden.co.uk/# (Dedicated Romany genealogy site)

HAMMERMEN

www.hammermenofglasgow.org / (Site of the hammermen of Glasgow)
www.hammermen.org/ (Site of the hammermen of Edinburgh)

www.troonayrshirefhs.org.uk/hammermen/index.html (Details of Irvine Hammermen, with actual names in old records)

HANGMEN & EXECUTIONERS

www.forum.familyhistory.uk.com/archive/index.php/t-12969.html (Capital punishment forum)
en.wikipedia.org/wiki/Category:English_executioners (List of English executioners)
www.capitalpunishmentuk.org/hangmen.html (English hangmen 1850–1964)
www.capitalpunishmentuk.org/hanging1.html (British & N.I. hangings 1735–1964)
www.from-ireland.net/hangings-1641-fermanagh/ (Fermanagh Irish hangings – 1641 rebellion)
news.bbc.co.uk/1/hi/uk/5035690.stm (BBC page about British hangmen)

LAWYERS, ATTORNEYS & SOLICITORS

www.innertemple.org.uk/index.php/history/admissions-database (The Inner Temple Admissions database)
search.ancestry.co.uk/search/db.aspx?dbid=8022 (Search the Law List 1843)
tinyurl.com/d4co7oq (Access to records at The National Archives)

LEATHER WORKERS, TANNERS & BARKERS (See also SKINNERS)

tinyurl.com/ces5sk6 (Browse Google's links to local tannery histories)
www.peaklandheritage.org.uk/index.asp?peakkey=20801521 (Web page about the Peak District leather and tanning industry)
www.british-history.ac.uk/search.asp?query1=tanner (Historical documents listing one or more tanners)
www.walsall.gov.uk/index/leisure_and_culture/leathermuseum/history_of_leather.htm (The Walsall district leather industry, with PDF files listing individual workers)
www.walsall.gov.uk/index/west_midlands_tanneries_1940.htm (West Midlands tanneries of the 1940s)
www.lyons-family.co.uk/Lyons/1915-lyons-francis-william/Whichelow/wichelow.htm (History of the Whichelow leather industry & tannery, with pictures)
www.freemenofnewcastle.com/tanners/index.html (Page of the Newcastle Tanners/ Barkers Guild)

LIGHTHOUSE KEEPERS

www.bellrock.org.uk/people/people_keepers.htm (Bell Rock lighthouse keepers 1811–1988)
www.nlb.org.uk/historical/research.aspx (Northern Lighthouse Board resources for researchers)
www.trinityhouse.co.uk/lighthouses/lighthouse_list/bishop_rock.html (Trinity House list of lighthouses)
www.genuki.org.uk/big/Lighthouses/ (Lighthouse personnel in England, Wales and the Channel Islands 1841–1910)
www.history.ac.uk/gh/lhouse.htm (Sources from the Guildhall Library)
www.nas.gov.uk/guides/lighthouses.asp (Guide to Scottish lighthouse records)
www.findmypast.co.uk/search/trinity-house-calendars/ (How to search the Trinity House calendars 1787–1854)

LOCKSMITHS

www.locksmithsregister.com/history.php (A history of locksmiths, with links)

MAGISTRATES

tinyurl.com/bn8z2b8 (Thousands of links to magistrates and other nationwide law links)

MARBLERS

www.uk-genealogy.org.uk/genuki/DOR/CorfeCastle/articles.html (Marblers of Corfe Castle)

MARINERS / MERCHANT NAVY

www.welshmariners.org.uk/ (Welsh mariners database and resources)
www.welshmariners.org.uk/search.php (Search for Welsh mariners here)
www.crewlist.org.uk/othersites.php (CLIP mariner's research website)
www.swanseamariners.org.uk/ (Swansea mariners)
www.glamorganfamilyhistory.co.uk/maritime/MMWHITBY.html (Whitby mariners and wives 1851)
tinyurl.com/blxuw5q (Research guide for tracing merchant seamen)
www.genuki.org.uk/big/MerchantMarine.html (Site containing lots of maritime resource links)

www.red-duster.co.uk/chart%20room.htm (Merchant navy information and links)
www.searcher-na.co.uk/merchant_navy_records.htm (Guide to official records and what you will find in them)
www.mna.org.uk/ (Merchant Navy Association homepage)
www.swanseamariners.org.uk (Swansea maritime records including sailors, ships and much more)
www.welshmariners.org.uk/ (Welsh mariners and naval database)
www.mariners-l.co.uk/UK19thCSeamen.html (Website of the Mariners Mailing List)
www.mun.ca/mha/ (Maritime history website based in Canada)
members.societe-jersiaise.org/alexgle/JMSBS.html (Jersey-based Merchant seamen resource site)

MATHEMATICIANS

www-history.mcs.st-and.ac.uk/Miscellaneous/EBlist.html (Encyclopedia Britannica's biographies of mathematicians and scientists)
www-history.mcs.st-and.ac.uk/External/Westfall_list.html (Early 16th and 17th century mathematicians' archive)
www-groups.dcs.st-and.ac.uk/~history/Davis/index.html (Women in the British Isles, 1878–1940, who graduated as mathematicians – search by name or university)
turnbull.mcs.st-and.ac.uk/~history (Mathematical Archives database)

MERCHANTS

www.new.fibis.org/archives/552 (Free merchants in India 1720–1780)
www.uk-genealogy.org.uk/genuki/DOR/CorfeCastle/articles.html (Stone Merchants of Corfe Castle)
www.danbyrnes.com.au/merchants/ (Chronologically lists merchants, bankers and related history from earliest times to 2002)
dbwebtest.liv.ac.uk/merchants/ (Liverpool merchants' and ship owners' database)

MILLERS

tinyurl.com/cv4omz2 (Genuki's links to local mills and millers)
www.windmillworld.com/uk/yorkshire.htm (Yorkshire windmills)
www.millsarchivetrust.org/index.php/ (Website designed to share records and history relating to traditional mills and milling)

www.hertfordshire-genealogy.co.uk/data/projects/bernardsheath/booklet-windmills.htm (Windmills of St Albans in the 1600s and 1700s)
www.norfolkmills.co.uk/windmills.html (Norfolk mills and millers)
www.suffolkmills.org.uk/archivewindmills.html (Suffolk mills page)
www.windmillworld.com/index.htm (Windmill World – lots of links and information)

MINERS, MINING & QUARRYING

www.cmhrc.co.uk/site/disasters/ (Coalmining accidents and deaths database)
www.leadminingmuseum.co.uk/home.shtml (Scottish lead and gold mining)
tinyurl.com/chwctte (Peruse mining links of all kinds at Genuki)
www.welshmines.org/links/l_rschr.htm (Resources for Welsh mining research)
www.dmm.org.uk/names/d1920-29.htm (List of Northern mine accidents)
www.cmhrc.pwp.blueyonder.co.uk/lodisalp.htm (Alphabetical list of mining disasters in Britain)
www.welshcoalmines.co.uk/DisastersList.htm (List of mining accidents where there were five or more fatalities)
www.scottishmining.co.uk/5.html (Scottish mine accidents and disasters)
www.mining-memorabilia.co.uk/Links.htm (Lots of mining links)
www.genuki.org.uk/search/ (Type the word 'coal' into this Genuki search engine to access thousands of UK and Ireland coal mining resources)
www.cmhrc.pwp.blueyonder.co.uk/ (Coal mining resource centre including names of those involved in pit disasters)
www.nmrs.org.uk/ (Northern mine research society)
www.pdmhs.com (Peak District Mines Historical Society)
www.welshmines.org/ (Welsh Mines Society)
www.welshcoalmines.co.uk/ (Welsh coal mine page with links)
www.mining-memorabilia.co.uk (Website of the National Mining Memorabilia Association)
www.dmm.org.uk/mindex.htm (Website of the Durham Mining Museum with lots of links and resources)
www.pznow.co.uk/historic1/tin.html (Information on the tin miners of Cornwall and associated workers)
www.bbc.co.uk/nationonfilm/topics/tin-mining/ (BBC Cornish tin mining web page with film clips)
www.cmhrc.co.uk/site/disasters/ (Database of mining disasters & deaths)
www.ncm.org.uk (National Mining Museum website)
www.museumwales.ac.uk/en/bigpit (National Mining Museum of Wales)

Miners at the shaft top at Woodhorn Colliery, Northumberland, in the 1930s.

www.scottishminingmuseum.com/ (Scottish Mining Museum)
www.emr.gov.yk.ca/mining/placermining.html (Yukon gold mining resources)

MUSICIANS

www.bios.org.uk/ (Website of the British Institute of Organ Studies)
www.musicweb-international.com/garlands/alphabetA.htm (Alphabetical index of music composers)
www.wcom.org.uk/template.php?whichPage=history (Worshipful Company of Musicians web page)

NURSES & MIDWIVES

tinyurl.com/bwjtyz3 (Links to thousands of genealogical records relating to hospitals throughout the UK)

www.nationalarchives.gov.uk/records/looking-for-person/britisharmynurse.htm (NA military nursing archives)

www.nationalarchives.gov.uk/records/research-guides/british-army-nurses.htm (More NA military nursing resources)

www.nationalarchives.gov.uk/records/looking-for-person/royalairforcenurse.htm (Royal Air Force nursing records at the NA)

museumofthemind.org.uk/collections/archives (Bethlem Hospital archives)

rcnarchive.rcn.org.uk/archive-browse/RCN (Access to the Royal College of Nursing archives)

www.scarletfinders.co.uk/ (Military nursing website)

www.nursing.manchester.ac.uk/ukchnm/ (Website of the United Kingdom centre for the history of nursing and midwifery)

www.nationalarchives.gov.uk/records/research-guides/civilian-nurses.htm (National Archive civil nursing records)

PAPERMAKERS

archiveshub.ac.uk/features/feb08.shtml (Lots of papermaking resources)

www.papermakers.org.uk/ (Growing database of papermakers)

tinyurl.com/c3hlzat (Papermakers of Hatfield)

tinyurl.com/d3mk884 (Extracts from Paper Mills and Paper Makers in England 1495–1800)

tinyurl.com/cp2p3bx (Early 19th-century papermakers)

www.genuki.org.uk/big/wal/Paper.html (Welsh papermakers and paper mills 1700–1900)

PARISH CLERKS, SEXTONS & CHURCHWARDENS

wsom-opc.org.uk/ (Somerset Parish Clerks genealogy site)

www.genuki.org.uk/search/ (Type 'Churchwardens' into the Genuki search page to access over 1,200 records sources)

www.sussex-opc.org/index.php?t=marriage&no=11 (Sussex parish clerks)

www.lan-opc.org.uk/registers.html (Lancashire parish clerks project)

steve.pickthall.users.btopenworld.com/pci/4.html (Alphabetical lists of parish clerks located by county)

www.genuki.org.uk/cgi-bin/htsearch?words=churchwardens&method=and&format=
builtin-short&matchesperpage=20&sort=score&config=genuki (If this long
address seems daunting, simply type the word 'Churchwardens' into the Genuki
search page)

PHOTOGRAPHERS

tinyurl.com/bo4oo25 (Links to various lists of photographers)
tinyurl.com/c629xz2 (Browse Genuki's links to local photographer references)
www.victorianphotographers.co.uk/ (Database of UK and Eire photographers
1840–1940)
www.iowphotos.info/ (Isle of Wight photographers database)
findingphotographers.homestead.com/files/FF-Index.htm (Global resources for finding
photographers)
www.betterphoto.com/forms/linkAll.asp?catID=2 (Biographies of individual
photographers)
www.rogerco.freeserve.co.uk / (Illustrated website of Victorian and Edwardian
photography and photographers)
www.rogerco.freeserve.co.uk/victoria.htm (Selective lists of British photographers by
location)
www.thornburypump.myby.co.uk/PI/index.html (Database to enable the dating of
old photographs by photographer's name. There are also biographies of
photographers)
www.cartes.fsnet.co.uk/photo/azlist2.htm (Lists of photographers operating in Bristol
1852–1972)
www.edinphoto.org.uk/2/2__professional_photographers.htm (Lists of Edinburgh
photographers from 1839 onwards)
www.genuki.org.uk/big/wal/AberPhotos.html (Aberystwyth photographers 1857–
1900)
www.feldgrau.com/wsskb.html (German photographers in World War II)

PILOTS (AEROPLANE)

www.faa.gov/licenses_certificates/airmen_certification/interactive_airmen_inquiry/
(Search Airmen certificates)
www1.airliners.net/aviation-forums/general_aviation/read.main/343657/ (Airline Pilots
database)
www.gapan.org/ruth-documents/guild-news/75th%20anniversary%20booklet.pdf
(Guild of Air Pilots and Air Navigators, with history)

www.nationalarchives.gov.uk/records/combat-reports-ww2.htm (Search WWII combat reports of air squadrons from the NA)
www.airsciences.org.uk/archives.html (Farnborough Air Trust, Library and Archives)

PILOTS (MARINE)

www.impahq.org/ (International Marine Pilots Assn.)
www.pilotmag.co.uk/category/history/page/2/ (Marine Pilot online history magazine)
http://www.isle-of-wight-fhs.co.uk/articles/cpilot.html (Cowes, Isle of Wight, pilots list 1808)
www.ukmpa.org/ (Website of Maritime Pilots Association)

POETS

gerald-massey.org.uk/ (Lists of some lesser-known Victorian poets)
www.encyclo.co.uk/define/Elizabethan%20Poets (Elizabethan poets)
www.poetsgraves.co.uk/b.htm (Biographies and burial places)

POLICE (CIVIL & TRANSPORT)

tinyurl.com/bn8z2b8 (Thousands of links to nationwide police records and resources)
www.policememorial.org.uk/index.php?page=scottish-roll-of-honour (Scottish Police Roll of Honour)
www.nationalarchives.gov.uk/records/research-guides/royal-irish-constabulary.htm (Royal Irish Constabulary records at The National Archives)
www.nationalarchives.gov.uk/records/research-guides/transport-police.htm (Transport Police Records)
www.genuki.org.uk/search/ (Type 'police' into this website to find hundreds of UK and Irish police records)
www.nationalarchives.gov.uk/records/research-guides/metropolitan-police.htm (Metropolitan Police records held at The National Archives)
www.met.police.uk/history/ (Metropolitan Police site with history, links, etc.)
www.genuki.org.uk/big/Police.html (UK police research resources and links)
www.policehistorysociety.co.uk/ (UK police history site)
www.policememorial.org.uk/index.php?page=english-roll-of-honour (Rolls of honour of police who died in the course of their duty)
www.essex.police.uk/memorial/ (Essex Police Memorial Trust website)
homepage.ntlworld.com/jeffery.knaggs/l0101a.html (List of residents in Police Section House, 82 Charing Cross Road, Westminster, in 1901)

www.historybytheyard.co.uk/family_history.htm (London police family history page with useful links)
www.oldpolicecellsmuseum.org.uk/index.aspx (Police Museum website, Brighton)
eis.bris.ac.uk/~hirab/smp2.html (A website researching British members of the Shanghai Municipal Police 1854–1943)

POST OFFICE

www.postalheritage.org.uk/ (British Postal Museum & Archives)
www.genuki.org.uk/big/Indexes/POST.txt (Select list of Post Office workers from GPO records)
www.btplc.com/Thegroup/BTsHistory/BTgrouparchives/index.htm (Archives of BT and its predecessors from the early 1800s onwards)

POTTERY WORKERS

tinyurl.com/cpxbgju (Browse Google's links to potters and potteries)
www.antiquepottery.co.uk/Manufacturers.htm (List of antique pottery manufacturers)
www.thepotteries.org/allpotters/ (Database of over 1,500 potters located by name, date or location of factory)
www.thepotteries.org/allpotters/index_alpha.htm (Alphabetical historical list of Stoke on Trent potters)

PRISON STAFF (see also LAW & ORDER)

tinyurl.com/bmmck5l (How to find Holloway prison officers' records)
tinyurl.com/bulgs52 (Newgate prison staff records)
www.prisonsmemoryarchive.com/ (Prison interview with staff, prisoners & others connected with the Maze and Long Kesh prisons and Armagh gaol during the Troubles in Northern Ireland)
blacksheepancestors.com/uk/ (Misc. prison and criminal genealogy links)
www.hertfordshire-genealogy.co.uk/data/census/census1881-prison.htm (List of prison staff at St Albans, 1881)
www.annbarrett.co.uk/category/prison/ (Isle of Wight prison records)

PUBLICANS & INNKEEPERS

tinyurl.com/kobswt2 (Lots of links to help you find publicans and licensed victuallers)

www.historicaldirectories.org/hd/ (Search trade directories for UK towns here)
www.buckscc.gov.uk/bcc/archives/Public_houses.page (Buckinghamshire publicans)
www.genuki.org.uk/search/ (Type 'publican' or 'innkeeper' separately for access to hundreds of regional records listing these occupations)
www.sfowler.force9.co.uk/page_12.htm (Pub history page with links to other sites)
www.midlandspubs.co.uk/ (Midlands pubs and breweries)
tinyurl.com/c5a5nu9 (Details of holdings of the Scottish Licences Mutual Insurance Association Ltd, Glasgow)

RAILWAY WORKERS

www.lner.info/ (LNER Encyclopedia site)
tinyurl.com/d2hfwdl (The National Archives guide to tracing railway ancestors)
tinyurl.com/bvla8n9 (Links to trade union and other railway records)

2-4-0T locomotive no 3049, cica 1880, Derbyshire.

www.railwayancestors.org.uk/ (Railway Ancestors family history society)
www.nrm.org.uk/ (National Railway Museum site)
www.rchs.org.uk/trial/gwpf.php?wpage=home (Website of the Railway & Canal Historical Society)
www.trap.org.uk/ (Site with resources for tracing railway archives)
www.lnwrs.org.uk/ (London and North Western Railway website, with lots of resources including staff history databases)
www.midlandrailwaystudycentre.org.uk/Staff_detailed.htm (Details of staff and service records held by the Midland Railway Study Centre)

ROYAL HOUSEHOLD EMPLOYEES

tinyurl.com/cczqq8b (Search Royal Household staff 1526–1924)
dfmgenblog.blogspot.com/2006/05/royal-household-1660-1837.html (Database of Royal Court Officers and Servants 1660–1837 – uses PDF files)
boards.ancestry.co.uk/topics.royalty.links/mb.ashx (Links to Royal Household staff genealogy)

SCIENTIFIC INSTRUMENT MAKERS

historydb.adlerplanetarium.org/signatures/ (Search the Webster's Instrument Makers database)
www.wcsim.co.uk/ (Website of the Worshipful Company of Scientific Instrument Makers)

SCRIVENERS

www.scriveners.org.uk/ (Website of the Worshipful Company of Scriveners)
www.british-history.ac.uk/source.aspx?pubid=152 (Historic papers of the Scriveners Company 1357–1678)

SERVANTS

tinyurl.com/cgrqqfn (Emigration, Indentured services database)
search.ancestry.co.uk/search/db.aspx?dbid=49090 (Search for Bristol servants)
www.virtualjamestown.org/indentures/search_indentures.html (Database of servants sent to foreign plantations 1654–1686)
www.pricegen.com/immigrantservants/about.htm (Immigrant servants' database)
search.ancestry.co.uk/search/db.aspx?dbid=49090 (Bristol register of servants)

SILK WORKERS

www.wcml.org.uk/wcml/en/contents/trade-unions/silk-workers-unions/
(Trade records)

SKINNERS (See also LEATHER WORKERS)

www.skinnershall.co.uk/history/history.htm (History of the Skinners Company)
tinyurl.com/d4ahpre (Worshipful Company of Skinners records)
www.electricscotland.com/history/industrial/industry16.htm (Scottish Skinners/
leather makers)

SLAVE WORKERS, OWNERS & FREED MEN

tinyurl.com/cbp9ttu (Records of slaves and slave owners at The National Archives)
search.ancestry.co.uk/search/db.aspx?dbid=1129 (Search Slave Registers in the British
Dependencies)
www3.hants.gov.uk/archives/hals-collections/slavery-records.htm (Hampshire slave
records)
tinyurl.com/cbju3br (Liverpool Record Office site)
tinyurl.com/d6nwj8c (Bristol slavery connections)
tinyurl.com/d6u4x7l (BBC article about the church's involvement in slavery)
www.genuki.org.uk/search/ (Type in the word 'slavery' to access almost 500 research
resources)
www.liverpoolmuseums.org.uk/ism/ (International Slavery Museum website)
www.bbc.co.uk/history/familyhistory/get_started/caribbean_01.shtml (BBC guide to
Caribbean plantations and other genealogy records)

SQUAREMEN & SQUAREWRIGHTS

www.irvinetrades.org/wrightsandsquaremen (Scottish Squaremen)
en.wikipedia.org/wiki/The_Corporation_O%E2%80%99_Squaremen (Corporation of
Squaremen info)
squaremen.com/ (Corporation O' Squaremen site)
www.rootschat.com/forum/index.php?topic,226214.0.html (Page explaining what a
squarewright was)
www.phm.org.uk/keemu/display.php?irn=11368 (Squarewrights' flag and banner)

STEAM ENGINE MANUFACTURERS

en.wikipedia.org/wiki/List_of_locomotive_builders (Wikipedia's list of worldwide steam locomotive builders)

www.geog.port.ac.uk/lifeline/sem_db/sem_db_home.html (Home page of the Steam Engine Makers database)

STRAW INDUSTRY WORKERS

www.lutonculture.com/uploads/documents/1339774056_HatIndustry.pdf (Luton straw hatters)

www.hertfordshire-genealogy.co.uk/data/occupations/straw-plait-1851.htm (Southern counties straw plait dealers 1851)

www.hertfordshire-genealogy.co.uk/data/occupations/straw-plait.htm (Website about the straw plait industry, Hertfordshire)

www.hertfordshire-genealogy.co.uk/data/answers/answers-2001/ans-0135-austin.htm (About straw splitting)

SUGAR REFINERS & BAKERS

www.mawer.clara.net/allsources.html (Lots of links to sugar refiners and bakers resources)

www.mawer.clara.net/intro.html (A database of some of those involved in the UK sugar refining industry – 16th to 20th centuries)

TALLOW MANUFACTURERS

tinyurl.com/bq4eykz (Hundreds of links to directories and town guides mentioning tallow makers)

www.hertfordshire-genealogy.co.uk/data/projects/bernardsheath/booklet-tallow-works.htm (Tallow works at Bernard's Heath)

TELECOMMUNICATIONS

strowger-net.telefoonmuseum.com/tel_hist_hull.html (About the Hull Telephone Company)

www.btplc.com/Thegroup/BTsHistory/BTgrouparchives/index.htm (Archives of telecommunications from the early 1800s onwards)

THEATRE & GENERAL ENTERTAINERS

www.str.org.uk/notebook/archive/index.html (Society for Theatre Research)

www.bl.uk/theatrearchive (Theatre Archive Project)

www.elta-project.org/theme-elta.html (East London Theatre archives)

www.bristol.ac.uk/theatrecollection/bristol.html (Bristol Theatre Collection)

www.theatrerecord.org/information/trstory.html ('Theatre Record' online)

math.boisestate.edu/gas/whowaswho/index.htm (D'Oyly Carte Opera Company index of performers 1875–1982.

www.hertfordshire-genealogy.co.uk/data/census/census1881-entertainers.htm (List of Hertfordshire entertainers 1881)

www.genealogyreviews.co.uk/enApr07theatre.htm (Commercial site selling a CD, Who's who in the theatre?)

www.old-liverpool.co.uk/theatres.html (Liverpool theatres and playbills)

www.bris.ac.uk/theatrecollection/ (Website of the University of Bristol Theatre Collection)

www.genuki.org.uk/big/wal/Theatres2.html (Welsh theatres 1844–1870, some personal names mentioned)

www.arthurlloyd.co.uk/Burials.htm (Burial places of music hall and variety artistes)

www.music-hall-society.com/ (Home site of the British Music Hall Society)

TRADE UNION RECORDS

www.wcml.org.uk/links/ (Trade union links and resources)

search.warwick.ac.uk/website?q=trade+unions (Lots of trade union links)

www.unionancestors.co.uk/ (Trace a union and find out more about it through this website)

UNDERTAKERS

search.ancestry.co.uk/search/db.aspx?dbid=1779 (Search Australian death indexes for undertakers' names)

www.hertfordshire-genealogy.co.uk/data/topics/t058-undertakers.htm (Short study of undertakers' records)

VETERINARY SURGEONS

www.veterinaryhistorysociety.org.uk/diary.htm (Veterinary History Society)

www.nationalarchives.gov.uk/nra/lists/GB-1510-RVC.htm (The Royal Veterinary College pages)

The National Union of General Workers was formed in 1916.
© 2014 Colin Waters Collection

www.rvc.ac.uk/About/Museums/Museum.cfm (Museum of Veterinary History website, with search facility)
trust.rcvs.org.uk/heritage-and-history/ (Royal College of Veterinary Surgeons website)

WATCHMAKERS

surnames.meaning-of-names.com/genealogy/watchmaker/ (A selection of links to watchmaker genealogy resources)
www.clockswatches.com/ (British and Irish clock and watchmakers)

WEAVERS

tinyurl.com/cy8omom (Database of Scottish weavers)
tinyurl.com/cuemz4d (Tring canvas weavers)
www.perthweavers.bravehost.com/ (Perth handloom weavers)

ORDERS & FRIENDLY SOCIETIES

Membership of Orders and Friendly Societies often played a large part in the lives of our male forebears. These organisations provided regular social activities as well as a means of support for dependents should hard times, injury or death fall upon the breadwinner. Because of variations in name, unofficial Orders bearing similar names to official ones, and various offshoots and schisms over the years, it is worthwhile searching through all of the headings below that have similar names to the one you are researching.

ALL ORDERS

tinyurl.com/cjqsewe (National Archive links – scroll down or use 'Search' to find the order you are interested in)

www.sfowler.force9.co.uk/page_23.htm (Web page dedicated to Friendly Society research)

www.exonumia.com/art/society.htm (A to Z international list of all fraternal Orders and Societies with links to some of the organisations listed)

home.freeuk.net/pastandpresent/chapter_xvi.htm (Armadale Works Friendly Society's page with references to the Free Gardeners, Ancient Shepherds, Rechabites and Freemasons)

ATHELSTAN

www.athelstan.org.uk/ (Masonic Order of Athelstan)

BUFFALOES (Royal Antediluvian Order of Buffaloes)

www.raobgle.org.uk/ (Grand Lodge website)

www.raobgc.org.uk/ (R.A.O.B. Grand Council)

www.britishpathe.com/video/r-a-o-b-dublin/query/poverty (Movie RAOB outing Dublin 1921)

FORESTERS

www.aoforestersheritage.com/Archive.html (Foresters Heritage Trust pages)

archiveshub.ac.uk/data/gb133-kdf?page=3 (Records of the Knutsford District Foresters)

tinyurl.com/cctwx8k (Gwent records)

tinyurl.com/cwxy6ak (Denbighshire Foresters)

tinyurl.com/c458dv8 (Court Powys records)

www.forestersfriendlysociety.co.uk/our-history.aspx (A history of the Order)
www.epsomandewellhistoryexplorer.org.uk/Foresters.html (Yorkshire Foresters
– illustrated site)

FREEMASONS

www.owf.org.uk/ (Order of Women Freemasons)
freemasonry.dept.shef.ac.uk/?q=resources_2 (About genealogical records held at the
Library and Museum of Freemasonry)
www.freemasonry.london.museum/ (Library and Museum of Freemasonry with family
history resources)
www.ugle.org.uk/ (Grand Lodge of England website)
www.irish-freemasons.org/ (Grand Lodge of Ireland website)
www.grandlodgescotland.com/ (Grand Lodge of Scotland website)
www.jerseymason.org.uk/craft_library.html (Channel Islands Freemasonry)
www.isle-of-man.com/manxnotebook/history/socs/fmason.htm (A history of
Freemasonry and Manx lodges)

GLADES

theraob0.tripod.com/theraob/id31.html (International Order of Ladies Glades website)

KNIGHTS HOSPITALLERS (ORDER OF ST JOHN)

www.knightshospitallers.org / (Official site of Knights Hospitallers of the Sovereign Order
of Saint John of Jerusalem Knights of Malta)
www.british-history.ac.uk/search.asp?query1=hospitallers (Links to historical
resources concerning the Knights Hospitallers)

KNIGHTS OF MALTA / RHODES

www.newadvent.org/cathen/07477a.htm (Knights of Malta)
www.orderofmalta.org.uk/ (Order of Malta)

KNIGHTS TEMPLARS

www.british-history.ac.uk/search.asp?query1=templars (Historical records and
resources concerning the Templars)
www.compulink.co.uk/~craftings/200years.htm (A history of the Knights Templars)

met.open.ac.uk/genuki/big/eng/bkm/Radnage/templars.html (List of Radnage Templars 1237–1557)
greatprioryofscotland.com/ (Order of the Temple, Scotland)
www.rosslyntemplars.org.uk/ (Rosslyn Templars, Scotland website)
www.crystalinks.com/templarsnews.html (Various historical articles and links)

MALTA

www.orderofmalta.org.uk/ (Order of Malta in Britain)

ODDFELLOWS

www.oddfellows.co.uk/site/content/archives.aspx (Oddfellows online archive site)
www.redmilearchive.freeuk.com/odd-fel.html (Oddfellows of Redmile, 1838–1920)
archiveshub.ac.uk/data/gb217lac-86 (Material held at Swansea archives)
archiveshub.ac.uk/data/gb222bmssioo (Material held at Bangor archives)
tinyurl.com/butbgzu (Newtown resources)
www.ioof.org/ (Home page of the Grand Lodge of Oddfellows)
boards.ancestry.co.uk/topics.organizations.ioof/mb.ashx (Genealogy links for Oddfellows)
www.isle-of-man.com/manxnotebook/history/socs/oddflws.htm (Web page devoted to the Oddfellows from a Manx point of view)

RECHABITES

tinyurl.com/brkw5sm (Rechabites, Westmorland District)
www.nationalarchives.gov.uk/nra/searches/subjectView.asp?ID=O37425 (Wales – NA resources)
tinyurl.com/blnulkj (Alloa links)
www.isle-of-man.com/manxnotebook/history/socs/rech_his.htm (A history of the Independent Order of Rechabites with some IOM names)
www.british-history.ac.uk/search.asp?query1=rechabites (Historical links to various Rechabite groups)
www.isle-of-man.com/manxnotebook/fulltext/rh1911/index.htm (Online book – *A record of the origin, rise and progress of the Independent Order of Rechabites*)
genuki.cs.ncl.ac.uk/DEV/Clovelly/Rechabites.html (List of Clovelly Rechabites 1925/6)
a-day-in-the-life.powys.org.uk/cym/cymdeith/cs_drinkt.php (Brecon Rechabitism)
www.archiveswales.org.uk/anw/get_collection.php?inst_id=32&coll_id=76310&expand= (Archives of Wales Rechabite records)

The Independent Order of Rechabites was founded in 1835 as part of the temperance movement. © 2014 Colin Waters Collection

WATER RATS

www.gowr.net/ (Charitable Order with show-business members)

PARLIAMENTARY & POLITICAL RECORDS

Parliamentary records are useful to family historians whose ancestors have been involved in politics in any way, or have become entangled in affairs where government involvement took place. Hansard – the reports of parliamentary proceedings, the Parliamentary archives and the government's oral history collection are accessible from the UK Houses of Parliament website. Mayors and local councillors are often listed on boards in town halls and council offices. A few examples of such lists found on the Internet are given below and those for other places can be found using any search engine.

CHARTIST MOVEMENT

www.chartists.net/Chartist-archives.htm (Researching Chartists at The National Archives)
archiveshub.ac.uk/features/apr08.shtml (Archives hub for Chartism)
tinyurl.com/bwnpsec (Page about the Chartist uprising in Newport)
www.chartists.net/ (Chartist ancestry site)

GOVERNMENT/PARLIAMENTARY RECORDS

www.leighrayment.com/commons/Acommons2.htm (House of Commons constituencies and MPs – 1600s to modern times)
www.theyworkforyou.com/mps/ (Modern MPs at various election dates)
www.nationalarchives.gov.uk/records/looking-for-subject/parliament.htm (Guide to researching UK Parliament records)
www.histparl.ac.uk/ (History of Parliament including the House of Lords)
www.parliament.uk/business/publications/parliamentary-archives/ (Catalogue of Parliamentary Archives)

INTERREGNUM & CIVIL WAR RECORDS

tinyurl.com/bqekvpz (Resources at The National Archives)
www.british-history.ac.uk/source.aspx?pubid=606 (Acts and Ordinances of the Interregnum, 1642–1660)
www.british-history.ac.uk/search.asp?query1=interregnum (Official records of the Interregnum and Civil War period)
www.british-history.ac.uk/search.asp?query1=civil+war (Specific records dealing with the Civil War in England)

www.british-history.ac.uk/search.asp?query1=Royalist+composition+papers (Access to various Royalist Composition records)

LOCAL POLITICIANS

www.origins.org.uk/genuki/NFK/places/n/norwich/mayors_and_sheriffs.shtml (Norwich Mayors, Lord Mayors and Sheriffs 1835–1990)

www.huntingdontown.gov.uk/former-mayors (Huntingdon Mayors, 1729 to present times)

www.genuki.org.uk/big/eng/NTT/Nottingham/Mayors.html (Nottingham Mayors 1302–1749)

freepages.genealogy.rootsweb.com/~mrawson/mayors2.html (Dover Mayors 1606–1665)

freepages.genealogy.rootsweb.com/~mrawson/mayors.html (Maidstone Mayors 1649–1721)

www.genuki.org.uk/big/eng/YKS/Misc/Transcriptions/WRY/PontefractMayors.html (Pontefract Mayors 1484–1883)

www.genuki.org.uk/big/eng/DUR/GatesheadHistory/Ch11.html (Gateshead Mayors 1835–1973)

met.open.ac.uk/genuki/big/eng/BKM/Buckingham/bailiffs.html (Buckingham Bailiffs and Mayors 1513–1842)

www.genuki.org.uk/big/eng/YKS/Misc/Transcriptions/NRY/ScarboroughBailiffs.html (Scarborough bailiffs 1600–1810)

www.wiganworld.co.uk/stuff/wig1889p6.php?opt=wig1889 (Rectors and Mayors of Wigan 1245–1888)

www.british-history.ac.uk/report.asp?compid=45561 (Mayors and Sheriffs of London 1198–1470)

MAGNA CARTA

www.britainexpress.com/History/medieval/magnacarta-trans.htm (A translation of King John's agreement with the barony signed in 1215 that was seen at the time as a Bill of Rights for his citizens)

en.wikipedia.org/wiki/Magna_Carta (Wikipedia's comprehensive guide to the Magna Carta, with links)

OATH ROLLS

www.foda.org.uk/oaths/intro/introduction1.htm (Devon Oath Rolls)

www.bucksas.org.uk/rob/rob_11_3_109.pdf (Buckinghamshire Oath Rolls)

www.nationalarchives.gov.uk/records/research-guides/oath-rolls.htm (Oath Rolls held by The National Archives)

www.foda.org.uk/oaths/intro/introduction15.htm (Devon Oath Rolls 1723, with names of those found in them)

POLL BOOKS

tinyurl.com/d39swry (Genuki's links to thousands of resources mentioning poll books)

www.british-genealogy.com/books-records/pollbooks.html (General guide to using poll books)

www.thedorsetpage.com/genealogy/info/poll_book.htm (Names in Dorset poll books 1807)

abacus.rabancourt.co.uk/bedfordshire-pollbook-1784 (Bedfordshire poll books 1784)

www.thegenealogist.co.uk/nameindex/productinfo.php?id=815 (Poll book records – pay to view)

PROTESTATION ROLLS 1641

www.witheridge-historical-archive.com/taxes.htm (Protestation Rolls and early taxes)

www.brinsmead.net/sometax.htm (Somerset Protestation Rolls)

www.opcdorset.org/ChideockFiles/ChideockProtestation1641.htm (Chideock P.R.s from 1641)

tinyurl.com/c3za2gk (All about Protestation Oath Returns/Oath of Allegiance – Nonconformist, including Ireland, with links)

www.genuki.org.uk/search/ (enter the word 'Protestation' into this Genuki search engine to find over nearly 600 resources countrywide)

PASSPORTS

Passports in the sense that we know them today were not introduced until 1915, but 'safe conduct' certificates were issued in the 15th century and records exist from at least the 18th century for more recent individual documents.

www.nationalarchives.gov.uk/catalogue/RdLeaflet.asp?sLeafletID=109 (National Archives research guide – old passport records)

www.movinghere.org.uk/galleries/roots/asian/migration/passports.htm (Passport records held at the British Library)
www.scan.org.uk/researchrtools/passports.htm (A small selection of old passports to view online)

PHOTOGRAPHY

Though experiments started earlier, the first useful photographs for genealogists were produced in the mid to late 1800s. As well as general historical information, the Internet provides expertise and services for the restoration and dating of old prints. A few examples are listed below. See also under **OCCUPATIONS**.

LANTERN SLIDES

www.bristol.ac.uk/theatrecollection/magic_lantern_slides.html (Magic Lantern slide collection web page)
www.magiclantern.org.uk/ (Magic Lantern Society site)

Workers at Darwen Mills, Lancashire, in the early 20th century.

PHOTOGRAPHY – GENERAL

www.rogerco.pwp.blueyonder.co.uk/ (Victorian and Edwardian photography with links to studios)

tinyurl.com/cl2ygl8 (Links to lists of Victorian and Edwardian photographers)

www.cartedevisite.co.uk/ (Lots of links and resources for researching photographers)

www.genuki.org.uk/search/ (Enter the words 'photographs' and 'photographers' separately into the search engine on this page to find thousands of photography pages linked to genealogy)

www.ted.photographer.org.uk/photohistory_origin.htm (An historic timeline of photographic processes)

www.oldukphotos.com/ (Free access website featuring old photographs of the UK)

PHOTOGRAPH DATING & RESTORATION

tinyurl.com/d8jcqmd (Date your old photos online – small fee payable)

www.thornburypump.myby.co.uk/PI/index.html (Database to enable the dating of old photographs by photographer's name. There are also biographies of photographers)

www.cartes.freeuk.com/time/date.htm (Tutorial on how to date old photographs)

tinyurl.com/coav4ev (All about restoring your old photos)

PLACE-NAMES

The origin of place-names is a fascinating area of study. Some of them relate to people who originally owned the land (e.g. Harkerside in the Yorkshire Dales, named after the Harker family). It is interesting to discover place-name links to our ancestors, though these are often likely to be found in most cases at a local level, in the names of geographical locations or farms.

ALL PLACES

www.genuki.org.uk/search / (Type 'place names' into this search engine to obtain thousands of references to place-name sites and references in Britain and Ireland)

www.englishplacenames.co.uk/ (Study of constituent parts of all place-names)

www.rampantscotland.com/placenames/placenames1.htm (Scottish place-names around the world)

BRITAIN – GENERAL

en.wikipedia.org/wiki/List_of_generic_forms_in_place_names_in_the_United_
Kingdom_and_Ireland (Etymology of British place-names)
www.ashton-under-lyne.com/placenames.htm (A list of odd and unusual
place-names)
www.gazetteer.co.uk/ (Gazetteer of British place-names)
www.gazetteer.co.uk/gazmap1.htm (Map showing old county names of Britain)
www.daelnet.co.uk/placenames/ (Yorkshire place-names)
www.catholic-history.org.uk/latin_names.htm (Latin British place-names with modern
equivalent)
www.countrylovers.co.uk/places/placnams.htm (Place-names and their changes
throughout Norse, Anglo-Saxon, Latin and Norman periods of history)
www.fatbadgers.co.uk/Britain/places.htm (Changes in place-names throughout
British history)

ENGLAND & ENGLISH REGIONS

cornish-place-names.wikidot.com/ (Cornish place-names)
www.nottingham.ac.uk/ins/placenamesociety/index.aspx (English place-name
society page)
www.krysstal.com/londname.html (London place-names)
www.british-history.ac.uk/source.asp?pubid=3 (Gazetteer of London place-names)
www.englandsnortheast.co.uk/PlaceNameMeaningsAtoD.html (North-East England
place-names)
www.kentarchaeology.org.uk/Research/Libr/KPN/A/01/01.htm (Kent place-names
from the 1904–8 Ordnance Survey maps)
www.wirksworth.org.uk/DPI.htm (Locate Derbyshire place-names and parishes)

IRELAND

placename.ie/ (Irish place-name database)
www.irish-place-names.com/ (Irish places database based on 1851 census)
www.dublin1850.com/general/placenames.html (Meanings of Irish place-names)
www.wesleyjohnston.com/users/ireland/geography/placenames.html (Components
and evolution of Irish place-names)

ISLE OF MAN

www.isle-of-man.com/manxnotebook/fulltext/pn1925/index.htm (Isle of Man place-names)

www.george-broderick.de/iom_docs/iom_place-names.htm (Manx place-names)

SCOTLAND

www.domesdaymaps.com/Scottish+Place+Names+Index.htm (Scottish place-name index)

www.spns.org.uk (Scottish Place-Name Society)

www.orkneyjar.com/placenames/pl-isle.htm (Orkney place and location names)

www.shetland-heritage.co.uk/amenitytrust/placenames/placenames.html (Shetland Place-Name Trust website)

SCILLY ISLES

cornish-place-names.wikidot.com/isles-of-scilly (Scilly Isles names with dateline)

WALES

www.domesdaymaps.com/Welsh+Place+Names+Index.htm (Welsh place-name index)

www.behindthename.com/nmc/wel.php (The meanings of Welsh place-names)

PLAQUES, INSCRIPTIONS, DATESTONES, STATUES & SCULPTURES

Valuable information can be gleaned from plaques, inscriptions, date stones, statues and sculptures but because they are widely distributed, most were hard to trace before the Internet came on the scene. Below are a few examples of what may be found on the Net.

PLAQUES

www.english-heritage.org.uk/discover/blue-plaques/search/ (Search all English Heritage Blue Plaques)

www.oxfordshireblueplaques.org.uk/plaques/index.html (Oxfordshire Blue Plaques)

www.tameside.gov.uk/blueplaque (Tameside Blue Plaques)

www.plaqueguide.com/ (Interactive plaque finder map)
www.english-heritage.org.uk/discover/blue-plaques/ (Information and search facility for the Blue Plaques of London)
www.westminster.gov.uk/green-plaques-scheme (Westminster's Green Plaque scheme)
www.aberdeencity.gov.uk/education_learning/local_history/Commemorative Plaque.asp (Commemorative plaques in Aberdeen)
www.ulsterhistory.co.uk/plaques.htm (Ulster plaques with biographies)
www.manchester2002-uk.com/buildings/blue-plaques.html (Commemorative plaques in Manchester)

INSCRIPTIONS (GENERAL)

en.wikipedia.org/wiki/File:Ogham.Inscriptions.Cornwall.jpg (Map of Cornwall's inscription stones)
www.romanbritain.freeserve.co.uk/Rib.htm (Roman inscriptions in Britain)
runicdictionary.nottingham.ac.uk/links.php (Links to runic inscriptions)

DATESTONES

www.geograph.org.uk/search.php?i=34564509 (Details and images of date stones countrywide)
members.societe-jersiaise.org/alexgle/stonejsy.html (Jersey date stones register)
members.societe-jersiaise.org/alexgle/stonesark.html (Sark date stones)
www.angmeringvillage.co.uk/history/datestones.htm (Angmering, Sussex, village date stones)
www.kirkbymalham.info/KMI/kirkbymalham/datestone.html (Kirkby Malham date stones)
en.wikipedia.org/wiki/Datestone (Wikipedia page covering date stones, marriage stones and similar memorial tablets)

STATUES & SCULPTURES

www.pmsa.org.uk/ (Public Monuments and Sculpture Association)
www.publicsculpturesofsussex.co.uk/object?id=12 (Sussex sculptures database)
laststatues.classics.ox.ac.uk/ (Oxford University LSA database)
www.racns.co.uk/ (Public sculptures in Norfolk & Suffolk)
www.glasgowsculpture.com/db_works.php?fn=1&str=2&fld=&di=1&st=51 (Glasgow sculpture and statue database)

www.offbeat.group.shef.ac.uk/statues/database_uk.htm (Sporting statues project)
www.bbc.co.uk/leeds/citylife/sculpture_trail.shtml (Leeds statues and sculptures)

REFERENCE INFORMATION

Whether you are searching for an obsolete name, a technical tradesman's term, or require background facts for churches and buildings, the Internet can provide for your needs. There are also many free sites providing resources to make your ancestry search much easier and more interesting, including some that will translate foreign language websites into a readable (though not perfect) English form, others that will provide statistical data such as population figures, and those that will make calculations of various sorts.

ABBREVIATIONS

www.mcfedries.com/ramblings/email-jargon.asp (Guide to email and text language shortcuts)
www.hgs-online.org.uk/abbreviations.htm (Abbreviations of genealogical organisations and resources)
www.genuki.org.uk/big/eng/Indexes/NE_WarDead/Abbreviations.html (Abbreviations found on rolls of honour and war memorials)
www.nationalarchives.gov.uk/releases/2006/january/january1/abbreviations.htm (Abbreviations found in Government and Ministerial documents)
genuki.cs.ncl.ac.uk/Transcriptions/DUR/CensusAbbrev.html (Abbreviations found in censuses)
genuki.cs.ncl.ac.uk/DEV/Churchstanton/AbbrevRP.html (Some abbreviations found in parish records)
www.jonstorm.com/glossary/ (Computer jargon abbreviations – useful when consulting some websites)

BUILDINGS

www.victoriansociety.org.uk/advice/listed-buildings/ (About listed buildings)
www.britishlistedbuildings.co.uk/ (Listed buildings database)

www.buildinghistory.org/ (All you need to research old buildings)
www.astoft.co.uk/arch/index.htm (Architectural styles of old buildings with samples)

CURRENCY & OLD WEIGHTS & MEASURES

www.sizes.com/units/cran.htm (Old weights used by fishermen, etc.)
measuringworth.com/calculators/ppoweruk/ (Find the historic purchasing power of any amount of money for any date from 1264–2006)
www.xe.com/ucc/ (Universal modern currency converter)

DICTIONARIES

www.s9.com/ (Biographical dictionary – search over 30,000 obituaries of famous and notable people)
www.dictionarylink.com/ (Database of links to useful dictionaries of all kinds)
stommel.tamu.edu/~baum/hyperref.html (Massive collection of all kinds of dictionaries, glossaries, etc.)

GENEALOGICAL RESOURCES

www.ffhs.org.uk/education/courses.php (Federation of Family History Societies page listing genealogy courses and talks, free and payable)
www.genealogy-links.co.uk/html/freebies.html (Free resources for genealogists)
www.pharostutors.com/coursedescriptions.php#001 (Online courses in genealogy)

HANDWRITING, SCRIPTS & PALEOGRAPHY

genealogy.about.com/od/paleography/ (Links to reading, understanding and deciphering old handwritten documents)
www.nationalarchives.gov.uk/palaeography/where_to_start.htm (Tips on reading old documents)

LATIN

www.24carat.co.uk/frame.php?url=coininscriptions.html (Understand Latin inscriptions on coins, etc.)
www.genuki.org.uk/search/ (Type 'Latin' into this Genuki search engine to access tutorials, examples and translation resources)

www.quicklatin.com/ (Download free Latin translator)
www.worldlingo.com/en/resources/latin_dictionaries.html (Links to online Latin
dictionaries)

REGNAL YEARS

people.albion.edu/imacinnes/calendar//Regnal_Years.html (Calculate a date from a
regnal year)
www.combs-families.org/combs/reference/regnal.htm (A list of regnal years)

ROMAN NUMERALS

www.novaroma.org/via_romana/numbers.html (Convert modern numbers and dates
online to Roman numerals and vice versa)
www.freewebs.com/bluetrident/articles/%5BBT%5D_understanding_roman_
numerals.pdf (Detailed guide to understanding Roman numerals)

SOCIAL / LOCAL HISTORY

www.historymole.com/ (Historical event database)
www.fachrs.com/ (Family and Community Historical Research Society page)
www.bbc.co.uk/history/british/middle_ages/plague_countryside_01.shtml (Effects on
populations caused by the plague)
booth.lse.ac.uk/ (Charles Booth's searchable online archive of life and labour in London
1886–1903)
www.local-history.co.uk/Groups/index.html (List of local history societies in the UK by
location)

SURVEYS & STATISTICS

www.bristol.ac.uk/history/bhsp/ (British Historical Statistics Project)
www.statistics.gov.uk/ (The Office of National Statistics (ONS) website giving access to
government statistics both historical and modern)
homepage.ntlworld.com/hitch/gendocs/pop.html (Population statistics charts of
Great Britain and Ireland 1570–1931)
www.genuki.org.uk/big/Gazetteer/Statistics.html (Gazetteer statistics for Britain and
Ireland)

TRANSLATION

http://tinyurl.com/cos4j6k (Google's online translator sites listing)
www.microsofttranslator.com/ (Bing translator)
www.google.co.uk/language_tools?hl=en (Translation tools from Google)

WAGES / MONEY

projects.exeter.ac.uk/RDavies/arian/current/howmuch.html (Lots of historical money related sites)
www.wirksworth.org.uk/A04VALUE.htm (Resources to locate earnings for various classes of workers 1264–1954)

WAYBACK MACHINE

www.archive.org/index.php (A site featuring the Wayback Machine. Find old or extinct websites, images, music, texts, and much more)

WEATHER

www.metoffice.gov.uk/climate/uk/stationdata/ (Met Office historical weather data)
tinyurl.com/cq3nl3p (Weather history tables)
www.metoffice.gov.uk/learning/library/archive/collections (Met Office weather archives)
www.wirksworth.org.uk/A14WEATH.htm (A brief guide to historical British weather conditions 1600–1900)

RELIGION

It should not be assumed that our ancestors followed the same religion as ourselves and genealogists should always be prepared to check the records of other denominations. Roman Catholic and Church of England records are relatively easy to find and the links below should assist in finding records for some of the lesser known religions and sects, some of which were persecuted from time to time. These events caused large populations to flee and settle in new areas causing many problems when tracing individuals. Amongst these groups were the Huguenots, widely persecuted members of the Protestant Reformed Church of France and adjacent regions in the 16th and 17th centuries. Thousands were killed in Paris during the St Bartholomew's Day Massacre of 1572 and on subsequent occasions. Because Britain was a non-Roman Catholic society, many fled here where they settled and gradually became absorbed into British society.

The Quakers, otherwise known as the Society of Friends, began in Britain in the 17th century and gradually spread throughout the world as a peace-loving religious movement without creeds or hierarchical structures. Quaker records are invaluable to researchers as they date from early times and were often quite detailed. If the religion you are seeking is not listed here, try the websites listed under the 'Nonconformists (General)' subheading below where you will also find Oath Rolls of nonconformists swearing allegiance to the monarch. Also try the Genuki site listed below under the 'All Denominations' heading. See also under **OCCUPATIONS** for clergy, missionaries and church workers and officials.

ALL DENOMINATIONS

www.genuki.org.uk/search/ (Search here for records of any denomination in the UK or Ireland)

www.mdlp.co.uk/genweb/glossary.htm (Glossary of church terms found in old records)

www.ckfswebservices.com/churchdata/search.html (Search for records of all church denominations here)

www.hull.ac.uk/oldlib/archives/religion/western.html#monastic (Religious records of all kinds including those at the University of Hull)

www.complete-bible-genealogy.com/ (Genealogy of Biblical characters)

www.old-liverpool.co.uk/churches.html (Liverpool and Lancashire church and religion links)

www.bmdregisters.co.uk/ (All nonconformist records search site)

AMISH & ANABAPTIST

www.kindredtrails.com/RELIGION_Amish.html (US site)

www.kentarchaeology.org.uk/Research/Libr/Mls/MlsTovil/01.htm (Tovil, Kent burials)

tinyurl.com/bnw3ho3 (Amish community in Ireland)

BAPTISTS

tinyurl.com/bwar3n7 (Peruse Google's list of Baptist links)

www.lilyholtroad.co.uk/baptist-records/ (Benwick Baptist records)

lists.rootsweb.com/index/other/Religion/BAPTIST-CLERGY-N-CHURCHES.html (Baptist clergy links)

http://baptisthistory.org.uk/ (Baptist Historical Society page with family history link)
www.cyndislist.com/baptist.htm (Worldwide Baptist links)

BIBLE CHRISTIANS

tinyurl.com/cwzu9rh (Genuki's Bible Christian links)
genuki.cs.ncl.ac.uk/DEV/Shebbear/BibleChristians/index.html (Devon resources)

BRETHREN (ALL BRANCHES)

www.mybrethren.org/sitefram.htm (The My Brethren website)
www.plymouthbrethren.com/ (About the Plymouth Brethren)
www.victorianweb.org/religion/plymouth.html (Victorian Web – Plymouth Brethren)
www.calverley.info/pud_mor.htm (Fulneck United Brethren (Moravian) church records)
tinyurl.com/ckotwk8 (Browse Genuki's Brethren links)
www.cob-net.org/docs/groups.htm (Networking site with links to all the different
Brethren denominations)

CHURCH BUILDINGS

www.genuki.org.uk/big/churchdb/ (Search a database of British churches)
www.history.ac.uk/gh/briefs.htm (Guide to historical resources and parish indexes
concerning contributions to the rebuilding of St Paul's cathedral c1678)
www.genuki.org.uk/search/ (Type 'church' into this search engine to access records,
photographs and information from a staggering 40,000 individual web pages)
www.churches-uk-ireland.org/ (Search here for pictures and details of the church where
your ancestors were baptised, married or buried in Britain or Ireland)

CHURCH OF ENGLAND / IRELAND / SCOTLAND

theclergydatabase.org.uk/reference/list-of-bishops-in-england-and-wales-date/
(Searchable database of bishops, ministers and locations)
www.ireland.anglican.org/ (Church of Ireland website with a genealogy link)
archiver.rootsweb.com/th/index/CHURCHMEN-UK/ (Archives of the Churchmen
mailing list)
www.british-genealogy.com/resources/books/clergy/ (Book resources for researching
clergyman ancestors)
www.rootsweb.com/~onpresco/chatham.htm (Transcriptions of Argenteuil records
1820s–1880s)

www.europepresbytery.net/ (Church of Scotland European Presbytery website)
www.cofe.anglican.org/about/librariesandarchives/recordscentre/ (Church of England records portal)
www.lambethpalacelibrary.org/content/searchcollections (Search Lambeth Palace records)

CONGREGATIONAL

tinyurl.com/cmkmqrg (Browse Genuki's Congregational links)
www.woodbridgechurch.org.uk/Records/quay/quay.htm (Congregational BMD records, Woodbridge, Suffolk)
www.proni.gov.uk/introduction__congregational_union_of_ireland.pdf (Irish Congregational church records)
dwlib.co.uk/ (Dr Williams's nonconformist records)

CONVENTS

www.monlib.org.uk/papers/ebch/1999bellenger.pdf (Brussels nuns at Winchester1794–1857)
homepage.ntlworld.com/jeffery.knaggs/I0109c.html (Residents of St Vincent De Paul's Convent and Orphanage, 9 Lower Seymour Street, Portman Square, Marylebone, 1901)

EPISCOPAL

www.kindredtrails.com/RELIGION_Episcopal.html (Search US records)
www.aberdeencity.gov.uk/education_learning/local_history/archives/loc_churchrecords.asp#Episcopal (Episcopal records in Aberdeen)
tinyurl.com/6wwjn3b (RootsChat page for Episcopal Church records)

FRENCH EXILED CLERGY

www.le.ac.uk/lahs/downloads/ElliottvolumeLXIV-5sm.pdf (French exiled clergy in Leicestershire from 1792)
www.euppublishing.com/doi/abs/10.3366/inr.1984.35.1.41 (Read online about French exiled clergy in Scotland)
www.plantata.org.uk/papers/ebch/1999bellenger.pdf (Brussels nuns at Winchester 1794–1857)

HUGUENOTS

www.british-history.ac.uk/search.aspx?query1=huguenots (A good selection of Huguenot resources)
www.culturenorthernireland.org/article.aspx?art_id=973 (Irish Huguenots)
www.lerwill-life.org.uk/history/devhugs1.htm (Devon Huguenots)
georgianlondon.com/post/49464090911/the-london-huguenots (Huguenots in London)
tinyurl.com/ceu5rdc (Huguenot settlements outside London)
www.huguenotsociety.org.uk/uploads/docs/HuguenotFamilies_Contents.pdf (Huguenot names & resources)
www.huguenotsociety.org.uk/family/ (Guide to finding Huguenot family records)
www.aftc.com.au/Huguenot/Hug.html (List of Huguenot surnames)
www.huguenot.netnation.com/general/ (Huguenot Society web page)

JESUITS

www.sjweb.info/arsi/ (Worldwide Jesuit Archives)
www.jesuitarchives.ie/ (Irish Jesuit Archives)

JEWS

tinyurl.com/cmfnf3n (Lots of links from Genuki)
british-jewry.org.uk/ (British Jewry website)
www.jeffreymaynard.com/ (Lots of Anglo-Jewish links)
www.jewishgen.org/ (JewishGen website with many resources for tracing Jewish ancestry)
www.jgsgb.org.uk/ (UK Jewish Genealogical Society)
www.jgsny.org/ (USA Jewish Genealogical Society)
www.ajgs.org.au/ (Australian Jewish Genealogical Society)
www.jgstoronto.ca/ (Canadian Jewish Genealogical Society)
www.nljewgen.org/eng/index.html (Dutch Jewish Genealogy)
www.jewishgen.org/ (Worldwide Jewish Genealogy)
www.sephardicgen.com/spain_sites.htm (Sephardic Jewish genealogy in Spain with links to other world regions)
www.jewishgen.org/jri-pl/ (Polish Jews database)
www.sephardicgen.com/carib_sites.htm (Tracing Sephardic Jews in the Caribbean)

LUTHERANS

tinyurl.com/bvqork6 (Links to UK Lutheran resources)
www.lutheran.co.uk/ (Evangelical Lutheran Church website)
www.lutheransonline.com/lutheransonline/genealogy/ (US-based Lutheran genealogy site)

MENNONITES

www.kindredtrails.com/RELIGION_Amish.html (Includes also Anabaptist & Mennonite records)
www.mennonite.net/ (Official site of the Mennonite church with congregation search facility)

METHODISTS

tinyurl.com/c7wbk4r (Links to thousands of UK and Irish Methodist resources)
depts.drew.edu/lib/methodist/ (Accessing Methodist records at Drew University, USA)
www.kindredtrails.com/RELIGION_Methodist.html (Kindred Trails worldwide Methodist genealogy resources)
www.cyndislist.com/methodis.htm (Cyndi's list of Methodist family history resources)
www.isle-of-man.com/manxnotebook/famhist/v10n4.htm#91-92 (Methodist archives on the Isle of Man)
ulster.failteromhat.com/knock.php (Methodism in Ireland)

MONASTIC RECORDS

tinyurl.com/mmp7d9g (Guide to Medieval Cartularies of Great Britain and Ireland)
tinyurl.com/mpw732v (Links to thousands of abbey records and monastic archives)
www.british-history.ac.uk/catalogue.asp?gid=87 (Monastic and cathedral records)
yourarchives.nationalarchives.gov.uk/index.php?title=The_Dissolution_of_the_Monasteries_and_Chantries (Web page concentrating on the Dissolution of the Monasteries and Chantries in Britain and Ireland)

MORAVIANS

www.calverley.info/pud_mor.htm (Fulneck United Brethren (Moravian) church records)

MORMON

www.kindredtrails.com/RELIGION_LDS_Mormon.html (Lots of Mormon links)
familysearch.org/search (International Genealogical Index / Church of Latter Day Saints family search)

MUSLIM / ISLAM

genforum.genealogy.com/muslim/ (Muslim genealogy forum)
www.ezsoftech.com/akram/prophetslineage.asp (Prophets Lineage website)
www.stanford.edu/class/history18n/images/genealogy/ (Genealogy of Muslim Brothers website)
link-o-mania.com/main/islamic.htm (Islamic genealogy links)

NAZARENE

www.kindredtrails.com/RELIGION_Nazarene.html (Search Nazarene church records)
nazarene.org/ministries/administration/archives/ourarchives/record/display.html (Search for Nazarene church records' to access lots of UK resources)

NONCONFORMISTS (GENERAL)

tinyurl.com/c5h3szu (Links to lots of UK nonconformist record resources)
www.cornwall-opc-database.org/searchdb.php?dbname=baptisms_nc (Search for Cornish nonconformists)
http://www.genuki.org.uk/big/eng/LIN/nonconformist.html (Lincolnshire links)
www.genuki.bpears.org.uk/NBL/Newcastle/nonconf.html (Newcastle on Tyne resources)
www.bmdregisters.co.uk/ (Search for National Archives nonconformist records)

PENTECOSTAL

www.kindredtrails.com/RELIGION_Pentecostal.html (Search Pentecostal church records)

PRESBYTERIANS

tinyurl.com/dytdeet (UK wide resources from GENUKI)
www.presbyterianireland.org/ (Irish Presbyterian records)
genuki.cs.ncl.ac.uk/DEV/Presbyterians.html (Devon Presbyterians)
www.europepresbytery.net/ (Church of Scotland European Presbytery website)

QUAKERS (SOCIETY OF FRIENDS)

tinyurl.com/cn995l2 (Hundreds of links to Quaker resources)
www.qfhs.co.uk/ (Quaker Family History Society with research links)
www.leeds.ac.uk/library/spcoll/quaker/quakint1.htm (About the Quaker Archive
database at Leeds University Library)
west-penwith.org.uk/wpenq.htm (West Penwith Quakers)
www.quakersurnames.net/ (Katie's surname list – a selection of Quaker surname
resources)
www.ancestry.com/learn/library/article.aspx?article=2965 (Quaker records at Ancestry.
com)

ROMAN CATHOLICS / RECUSANTS / PAPISTS

tinyurl.com/d4wfmsv (Thousands of links to Roman Catholic resources)
www.catholic-history.org.uk/cfhs/ (Catholic Family History Society)
www.catholic-history.org.uk/crs/records.htm (Index to Catholic records)
www.catholic-library.org.uk/ (How to use the resources held by the Catholic Central
Library)
www.elizabethan-era.org.uk/elizabethan-recusants-recusancy-laws.htm (All about
Elizabethan recusants)
www.jacobite.ca/documents/16890320.htm (Scottish proclamation against Papists
1689)
history.hanover.edu/texts/ENGref/er87.html (Copy of the Act against recusants of 1593)
www.british-history.ac.uk/report.asp?compid=46295 (An act for removing Papists from
London 1688)
www.catholic-history.org.uk/nwchs/recushandbook.htm (Recusant historian's online
handbook)
genuki.cs.ncl.ac.uk/DEV/DevonMisc/Papists.html (List of Papists in Devon 1648)
www.genealogy-quest.com/collections/1716-langbaurgh.html (North Yorkshire
Papists 1716)

SEVENTH DAY ADVENTISTS

www.kindredtrails.com/RELIGION_Seventh_Day_Adventist.html (Search US records)
www.mundus.ac.uk/cats/41/1245.htm (About the Adventist archives)

SIKHISM

www.sikhsangat.com/index.php?/forum/12-gurbani-veechar-articles-history (Forum,
history and general topics)
ukpha.org/ (Sikhs at war)

SOCIETY OF FRIENDS (See under QUAKERS)

SWEDENBORGIAN

yourarchives.nationalarchives.gov.uk/index.php?title=Swedenborgianism
(NA resources)
www.swedenborg.org.uk/library (Swedenborg Society web page)
lists.rootsweb.com/index/intl/UK/UK-NEWCHURCH.html (Mailing list and archives for
the New (Swedenborgian) Church in the UK)

UNITARIANS

www.durhamrecordoffice.org.uk/Pages/UnitarianChurches.aspx (How to search for
records)
www.kindredtrails.com/RELIGION_Unitarian.html (Search Unitarian records)

SHIPPING INCLUDING PASSENGER & CREW LISTS

Passenger and crew lists can help to plot the movements of people around the world. In the case of sailors it was not uncommon for them to be away from home for one or more years, hopping off one ship when their duties finished and enlisting on another, often in some foreign port. On a smaller scale, crew lists exist of those working on transport vessels and on rivers, canals and waterways. Censuses should also be consulted as they list people who are on ships in ports on the night the census was taken. See also **EMIGRATION** and **OCCUPATIONS**.

ALL MARITIME RESOURCES

www.maritimearchives.co.uk/ships.html (A comprehensive list of all maritime resources including those listed in previous editions of this book)
www.hartlepoolsmaritimeexperience.com/ (Hartlepool maritime resources)
tinyurl.com/czxk5su (Royal Maritime Museum site)
www.lighthousesrus.org/index.htm (Lighthouses of the World – information and links)
www.cyndislist.com/ships.htm (Miscellaneous links to passenger lists, shipping, canal, river and waterway research subjects)
www.angelfire.com/de/BobSanders/Site.html (Navy and maritime research links and resources)
www.pbenyon.plus.com/Naval.html (Lots of naval and maritime resources)
www.mariners-l.co.uk/MarinersList.html (Mariners mailing list)

AUSTRALIA & NEW ZEALAND

www.anmm.gov.au/ (Australian National Maritime Museum)
www.maritimemuseum.co.nz/ (New Zealand National Maritime Museum)
www.emigrants.net.au/ (Passenger lists to Australia and New Zealand)
www.nzetc.org/tm/scholarly/tei-McN01Hist-t1-b1-d2.html (Crew of Capt Cook's Endeavour, 1770)

IRISH, SCOTTISH & WELSH

homepage.eircom.net/~navalassociation/picturegallery4.htm (Irish maritime and naval links)
www.commissionersofirishlights.com/ (Irish lighthouses website)
www.maritime-scotland.org.uk/ (Early Scottish maritime resource)
www.scottishmaritimemuseum.org/ (Scottish Maritime Museum)
www.museumwales.ac.uk/en/2327/ (Welsh maritime resources)

www.swanseamariners.org.uk/ (Swansea mariners site)
www.swanseamariners.org.uk/swanseamariners.php (Swansea ships and mariners database)
www.lof-news.co.uk/WOF.htm (Welsh Ore Carriers and Overseas Freighters)
www.scotlandsfamily.com/ships-passengers.htm (Scottish passenger list links)
www.olivetreegenealogy.com/ships/scotstousa.shtml (Scottish emigrant lists, including individual ships)
freespace.virgin.net/alan.tupman/sites/irish.htm (Lots of links to Irish passenger sources)

LIVERPOOL DEPARTURES

www.liverpoolmuseums.org.uk/maritime/ (Liverpool Maritime Museum)
immigrantships.n et/departures/lpool.html (Passengers departing from Liverpool 1772–1929)
www.old-liverpool.co.uk/captains.html (Liverpool ships, shipwrecks, passengers and crew)

NORTH & SOUTH AMERICA / CANADA ARRIVALS

www.collectionscanada.gc.ca/genealogy/022-908-e.html (Canadian immigration links)
www.bl.uk/eccles/pdf/immigration.pdf (About US immigration 1840–1940)
freepages.genealogy.rootsweb.ancestry.com/~northing/immig/usa_ships.html (USA & Canada ship arrivals)
www.germanroots.com/passengers.html (Links to trace arrivals at US ports from Europe)
retirees.uwaterloo.ca/~marj/genealogy/thevoyage.html (Canadian arrivals)
www.casahistoria.net/mimosa1.htm (Ship *Mimosa* carrying Welsh immigrants to Patagonia)

PASSENGER & CREW LISTS (INCLUDING LINKS & SEARCHES)

www.crewlist.org.uk/ (Crew List Project)
www.findmypast.co.uk/search/clip-crew-lists (Search crew lists 1861–1913)
tinyurl.com/8yj7gpz (Ships lists at Ancestry.com)
www.genealogylinks.net/uk/wales/all-wales/wales-ships.htm (Welsh passenger lists)
www.cyndislist.com/ships.htm (Links to passenger lists and other maritime sites)
rmhh.co.uk/passen.html (Lots of links to passenger and crew lists)

freespace.virgin.net/alan.tupman/sites/ships.htm (Passenger lists arranged by country and name of ship)

mayflowerhistory.com/mayflower-passenger-list/ (Passenger list of the *Mayflower*'s voyage to colonise USA – click names for biographies)

www.theshipslist.com/ships/passengerlists/index.htm (Lists of passengers 1700–1900, with various search facilities)

olivetreegenealogy.com/ships/toausp01.shtml (Miscellaneous passenger lists, with links to other genealogy subjects)

www.passengerlists.co.uk/search.htm (Search for war brides on passenger ships)

www.canadianwarbrides.com/passenger-lists.asp (War brides bound for Canada on passenger ships)

explorenorth.com/whalers/crew-prospect.html (Crew list of the whaling ship *Prospect*, of Whitby, 1788)

explorenorth.com/whalers/crew-volunteer.html (Crew list of the whaling ship *Volunteer*, of Whitby, 1772 and 1815)

SHIPS

www.lr.org/about_us/shipping_information/faqs.aspx (How to search Lloyd's shipping register)

www.genuki.org.uk/search/ (Type 'ships' into this search engine for over a thousand resources)

www.old-liverpool.co.uk/captains.html (List of Liverpool ships)

www.genuki.org.uk/big/Helena.html (Ships and residents of St Helena during Napoleon's imprisonment 1815-1821)

homepage.ntlworld.com/jeffery.knaggs/RNShips.html (1901 index of Royal Navy ships and their positions, captains, etc, at the 1901 census)

www.fleetairarmarchive.net/Ships/Index.html (Fleet Air Arm and other shipping links)

explorenorth.com/whalers/ships-whitby.html (List of Whitby whaling ships 1753–1837)

explorenorth.com/whalers/features/whalewrecks.htm (Details of shipwrecked whalers 1746–1907)

www.plimsollshipdata.org/ (Search Lloyd's Register for ships 1930–1945)

www.oceanlinermuseum.co.uk/ (Lots of resources for liners and container ships)

SHIP OWNERS & CAPTAINS

www.shipownersclub.com/about-us/history-of-the-club (Shipowners' Club website)
http://boards.ancestry.co.uk/localities.britisles.england.cul.general/277.2/mb.ashx
(Whitehaven ship owners in 1834 - Search)
www.genuki.org.uk/big/wal/NevillLlanelly.html (W. H. Nevill and the Llanelly Iron
Shipping Company)
explorenorth.com/whalers/features/whalecaptains1.htm (List of captains of whale
fishing ships)

SHIP BUILDERS & SHIP BREAKERS

www.fleetairarmarchive.net/Ships/Shipyards/Shipyards.html (British and worldwide
shipyards)
www.fleetairarmarchive.net/Ships/Shipyards/Scrapyards.html (Scrapyards and ship
breakers resources)
www.mariners-l.co.uk/WWIStandardBuilt.htm (WWI ships, shipbuilders and ship types)
en.wikipedia.org/wiki/Cammell_Laird (All about Cammell Laird ship builders, including
list of ships)
en.wikipedia.org/wiki/Harland_and_Wolff (Harland and Wolff history, photos and ships
list)
www.communigate.co.uk/ne/pallionshipyard/index.phtml (All about the Pallion
shipyards, with historic shipping photos)
en.wikipedia.org/wiki/Swan_Hunter (Swan Hunter history, ships and links)
www.bbc.co.uk/nationonfilm/topics/ship-building/background.shtml (History of the
North East shipbuilders)

SOUTH AFRICA

www.eggsa.org/arrivals/lists.html (SA Genealogical passenger list site)
www.searchforancestors.com/records/passenger_tosa.html (Search passenger lists
to SA).

TITANIC

www.encyclopedia-titanica.org/titanic_passenger_list/ (Passengers and crew of the
Titanic, plus other information about the ship and its voyage)

SOCIAL NETWORKING GENEALOGY SITES

There are a growing number of social network sites which you can use for finding and sharing information and as online communities for people with common interests.

www.facebook.com/pages/Genealogy/96653184251 (Using Facebook for genealogy)
www.geneabloggers.com/ten-people-genealogists-follow-twitter/ (Twitter genealogy blogs)
www.ebizmba.com/articles/social-networking-websites (Other social network site links to explore)

SPORTS & SPORTSMEN

There are literally thousands of websites dedicated to sport. These are just a few that genealogists may find useful.

boxrec.com/search.php (Boxing records search box)
www.en.wikipedia.org/wiki/List_of_world_records_in_athletics (lists of world records in athletics)
en.wikipedia.org/wiki/Cycling_records (Cycling records)
www.sportsrecords.co.uk/ (General sports records)
www.nationalfootballmuseum.com (National Football Museum)
www.natlsportsfoundation.com/museum.html (American Sports Museum)
www.nationalarchives.gov.uk/olympics/timeline.htm (National Archives sports web page)
www.genuki.org.uk/search/ (Type in the word 'sport' or any individual sport name, such as 'football', to access hundreds of British and Irish sporting documents and resources)
www.sportsrecords.co.uk/index.htm (Wide variety of sporting records and information)
www.sportsrecords.co.uk/rugbyunion/links.htm (Rugby Union links)
content-www.cricinfo.com/wisdenalmanack/content/current/story/almanack (Search Wisden Cricketer's Almanac)
www.ukathletics.net/supporters/gb-records/ (Athletics records)
www.horseracinghistory.co.uk/hrho/action/viewBrowse?search=Person&type =Trainer (Horse racing archives listing trainers, riders, breeders, etc)
www.nhrm.co.uk/ (Website of the National Horse Racing Museum)
www.all-athletics.com/ (Comprehensive athletics database)
www.databaseolympics.com (Olympics database)

STRAYS

In genealogical terms, strays are people born or normally living in one place who are found in official records elsewhere, often a census in another town. Many family history societies have compiled lists of strays in their own areas to aid genealogists who are looking for 'missing' members of any particular family.

tinyurl.com/calegcs (Browse thousands of links to genealogical strays)
www.ffhs.org.uk/projects/strays.php (The National Strays Index)
www.genuki.org.uk/big/eng/YKS/Misc/1/index.html (Yorkshire strays found elsewhere in 1851 and 1881)
www.msurman.freeserve.co.uk/www/pages/Glos%20Strays.htm (Gloucester boat people strays)
www.wirksworth.org.uk/C51STRY1.htm (Some Derbyshire strays)
www.anglo-scots.mlfhs.org.uk/ (Page containing database of Scottish strays)
www.originsnetwork.com/help/helpio-census1841.aspx (Irish strays, 1841 census)
www.genuki.org.uk/search/ (Enter the word 'strays' to access over 6000 nationwide sources)
romanygenes2.webeden.co.uk/#/strays/4527119321 (Romany strays)

SUPPLIES & SERVICES

Commercial supplies and services are quite easy to find on the Internet and this is only a small sample of the vast range available at the time of writing.

AUDIO SERVICES

www.rootschat.com/forum/index.php/topic,210049/prev_next,next.html (DIY audio services)
www.hotfrog.co.uk/Products/Audio-Tape-To-Cd (Audio transfer links)
www.preciousvoices.co.uk / (Professional transfer of precious family audio records on tape to CD)

BOOKS & CDs

www.genealogysupplies.com/index.php (Genealogy books, CDs and other resources)

www.gutenberg.org/wiki/Main_Page (A project to transcribe historic books, catalogues and other printed material of all kinds for display online)
www.my-history.co.uk/acatalog/ (Commercial online listing of books, software, etc, for family historians)
www.archivecdbooks.org (Commercial company transferring old books, records and directories to CD)

BOOKPLATES

www.bookplatesociety.org/ (Website of the Bookplate Society – collections, history, illustrations, buy and sell, etc.)

GENEALOGY SOFTWARE & SUPPLIES

www.genealogyreviews.co.uk/genealogysoftware.htm (Genealogy software reviews)
www.ukgid.com/links/software.html (A selection of computer genealogy programs to purchase)
www.genealogyprinters.com/index.php?refid=genealogyprinters2708%20042154 (Charts plus print supplies and services)
www.acorns2oaks.info/ (Professional printing of family trees and more)
www.GenealogySupplies.com (S & N Genealogy Supplies for mail order books, CDs and software)

MICROFILM / FICHE SUPPLIES

www.microfilm.com/ (All microfilm supplies)

SURNAMES

There are many sites and individual pages dedicated to researching individual surnames or for finding old records that contain a given surname. Some will contain worldwide references; others will have a bias towards, say, English or American families. It is always worth searching all sites regardless of their country of origin as many will refer to foreign national families who originated from Europe. American and Australian sites often contain historical family trees, references and facts that will not be found on British sites. In addition, nearly all the Subjects in this book will also yield surname lists.

ALL NAME SEARCHES & LINKS

www.surnamenavigator.org/ (Search for a surname using a dozen or so major search engines at once)

www.practicalresearchindexes.co.uk/16253/26323/index.html (Search list of names and locations taken from old postcards worldwide – fee payable)

www.digiserve.com/heraldry/surnames.htm (Lots of name resources, including regional and foreign names)

www.daddezio.com/genealogy/search/index.html (Surname search using various search engines)

surname.rootschat.com/sit-surnames.php (Search lists by initial letter)

www.surnameweb.org/ (General search tool or search by initial letter)

www.surnamefinder.com/ (Links to many surname resources)

resources.rootsweb.com/surnames/ (Search surnames by initial letter)

www.dmoz.org/Society/Genealogy/ (Search for any name, address, date, phrase, etc, on the web)

www.searchforancestors.com/quicksearch/ (Index of databases, with surname interests)

www.worldwidetopsites.com/sites/genealogy.html (Lists specialized surname search engines)

www.surnamedirectory.com/surname-index.html (Search for specialized sites for individual surnames)

www.genealogy-links.co.uk/html/search.html (Search engine with a British bias)

www.genuki.org.uk/search/ (Search lots of UK databases for any given name)

www.sfhg.org.uk/mipageA.html (Index to burial surnames found in Suffolk)

www.quakersurnames.net (A selection of Quaker surname resources)

www.youririshroots.com/index.php (Search for Irish surnames)

www.stevebulman.f9.co.uk/cumbria/jollie_carlisle_f.html (List of Carlisle residents 1811)

webs.lanset.com/azazella/cornish_database.html (Cornish databases, transcripts and specific name studies)

www.accessgenealogy.com/test/canada.cgi (Canadian surname search)

www.aftc.com.au/Huguenot/Hug.html (List of Huguenot surnames)

http://gbnames.publicprofiler.org (Search for origins of your surname)

www.censusdiggins.com/ (Vast array of specialist surname searches)

www.genealogytoday.com/names/origins/french.html (French surname search)

www.surnameweb.org/German/surnames.htm (Search resources for German surnames)

http://genealogy.about.com/cs/surname/a/spanish_names.htm (List of top 50 Spanish surnames, with genealogical links)

surnames.behindthename.com/names/usage/scandinavian (Scandinavian surname resources)

surnames.behindthename.com/php/search.php?terms=Dutch&title=Dutch+ Names&usage=yes (List of Dutch surnames and links)

SURNAME DISTRIBUTION MAPS

worldnames.publicprofiler.org/ (International surname mapper)

www.rootsmap.com/ (Commercial site offering surname distribution maps)

www.irishtimes.com/ancestor/ (Enter your Irish surname to obtain a free historical name distribution map)

en.wikipedia.org/wiki/Maps_of_American_ancestries (American origins maps)

NAME CHANGE RECORDS

http://www.adviceguide.org.uk/england/search.htm?query=name+change (Citizens Advice page)

www.deedpoll.org.uk/ (Details of the process of changing names by Deed Poll)

www.nationalarchives.gov.uk/familyhistory/name/default.htm (National Archives' advice on accessing name change records)

ONE NAME WEBSITES

www.ffhs.org.uk/members2/onename.php (List of societies that are studying a single surname)

www.one-name.org/ (Guild of One-Name Studies website)

TAXATION

Taxation records, particularly very old ones pertaining to specific areas, can be useful in providing names and locations. Locating them can be difficult, but several websites explain the history and whereabouts of taxation lists.

ALL TAXES

www.witheridge-historical-archive.com/taxes.htm (A page devoted to early taxes by type)

tinyurl.com/cft8mzy (Genuki's links to local and general tax records and resources)
www.nationalarchives.gov.uk/search/quick_search.aspx?search_text=Taxes (Links to all tax records held at The National Archives)
www.british-history.ac.uk/search.asp?query1=tax (Search here for historical tax records)
www.medievalgenealogy.org.uk/guide/tax.shtml (Historical guide and links regarding English tax records)
www.scan.org.uk/researchrtools/tax.htm (A selection of viewable old tax documents)

HEARTH TAX

tinyurl.com/d2fckte (Regional Hearth tax records)
www.nationalarchives.gov.uk/catalogue/RdLeaflet.asp?sLeafletID=233 (Records of medieval and early-modern taxation – 13th century-1689)
www.british-history.ac.uk/period.asp?period=7&gid=54 (Sourcing Hearth Tax returns)
www.maybole.org/history/Archives/hearthtax1691.htm (Ayrshire Hearth Tax records 1691)
www.wirksworth.org.uk/97-HTAX.htm (Wirksworth, Derbyshire Hearth Tax records)
www.hrionline.ac.uk/conisbrough/browse/hearthtax_1.html (South Yorkshire Hearth Tax Returns, 1672)

LAND TAX

media.nationalarchives.gov.uk/index.php/the-land-tax-1692-1963/ (NA online video)
www.uk-genealogy.org.uk/datafiles/landtaxsearch.html (Search returns of Owners of Land in 1873)
www.hertfordshire-genealogy.co.uk/data/occupations/land-tax-1863.htm (List of Land Tax commissioners for Hertfordshire in 1863, with source available for other areas)
http://www.great-harwood.org.uk/about/History/Documents/tax%20lists.htm (Great Harwood Land Tax record with names, 1800)
www.history.ac.uk/gh/landtax.htm (Land Tax records in the Guildhall Library)
genuki.cs.ncl.ac.uk/DEV/Otterton/LandTax1781.html (Land Tax records, Otterton, Devon, 1781)

POLL TAX & SUBSIDY ROLLS

tinyurl.com/cfpdnhx (Links to lots of local resources)
www.genuki.org.uk/big/eng/YKS/Misc/SubsidyRolls/YKS/SubsidyRolls1379Index.
html (Subsidy rolls 1379, with lists of names for Yorkshire)
www.british-history.ac.uk/report.asp?compid=36016&strquery=clergy (Taxation of the
Clergy and Poll Tax 1381)
www.exploregenealogy.co.uk/PollTaxMiddleAges.html (Poll tax in the Middle Ages)

SCOTTISH TAXES

www.scotsgenealogy.com/Resources/ScottishTaxationRecords.aspx (Guide to
miscellaneous old taxes including farm horse and clock taxes)
www.nas.gov.uk/guides/taxation.asp (Guide to old Scottish Tax records)

WINDOW TAX

www.sussexrecordsociety.org/bookw.asp?BookId=wtax900 (East Sussex window &
house tax database)
www.longparish.org.uk/history/windowtax.htm (Short description of the Window Tax
1696–1851)
www.headington.org.uk/oxon/people_lists/oxford_1696_window_tax/index.htm
(List of Window Tax payers in Oxford, 1696)

VILLAGES

Apart from the task of finding ancestors who lived in particular villages, the genealogist may even have difficulty in tracing the village itself – some have been absorbed by larger conurbations, while others have been abandoned or even lost altogether. The Internet is particularly useful in tracing these lost villages and in finding maps or other information that will be useful. Many present villages have their own community websites so it is always worth searching for them by name on the net.

BRITISH & IRISH VILLAGES

www.irish-tokens.co.uk/ir-towns.htm (Irish towns and villages and their county)
www.british-towns.net/ (British towns and villages network)
www.orion-arts.com/villages/ (Central link for individual village websites)

DESERTED & LOST VILLAGES

www.abandonedcommunities.co.uk/page39.html (Abandoned St Kilda)
en.wikipedia.org/wiki/List_of_lost_settlements_in_the_UK (List of deserted medieval and shrunken villages)
www.hunimex.com/warwick/warks_lost_villages.html (Deserted villages in Warwickshire)
www.cotswolds.info/blogs/deserted-villages.shtml (Deserted Cotswold villages)
www.bbc.co.uk/history/british/middle_ages/plague_countryside_01.shtml (Villages deserted because of the plague)
www.english-heritage.org.uk/daysout/properties/wharram-percy-deserted-medieval-village/ (Wharram Percy, North Yorkshire village deserted since 1500)
www.diplomate.freeserve.co.uk/gainsthorpe.htm (Lost Lincolnshire villages)
www.herefordshire.gov.uk/htt/1015.aspx (Villages lost without trace, plus general information on medieval villages)
www.abandonedcommunities.co.uk/ (Abandoned Communities website)

MODERN VILLAGES

www.ukvillages.co.uk/ (Search here for details of a modern village)

WARTIME & MILITARY RESOURCES

Service records of those who served in the forces are extremely valuable and can provide us with much personal information, even to the extent in some cases of describing the height, eye colour and other features of one of our ancestors. War grave records, regimental sites and those dealing with battles and war history in general are also worth looking at for snippets of information and sometimes anecdotes describing individual soldiers, sailors and air force personnel. An Act of Parliament passed on 6th February 1918, made servicemen over the age of 21 eligible to vote in their home constituency. A few of these lists, known as Absent Voters Lists, can be found online using the link below under World War I. Civilian and other records are also valuable and appear in abundance on the net. Samples of these are included below together with listings of sites relative to all wars and conflicts that may be of interest to family historians.

AFGHANISTAN CONFLICTS

www.garenewing.co.uk/angloafghanwar/ (About the Second Anglo-Afghan War 1878–1880)

members.tripod.com/%7EGlosters/FAfghan.htm (Officers killed in the Victorian Afghan conflict 1838–1842)

members.tripod.com/%7EGlosters/afghStaf.htm (Officers killed 1878–1880, with photographs)

members.tripod.com/%7EGlosters/afghcav.htm (Cavalry men killed 1878–1880, with photographs)

members.tripod.com/%7EGlosters/afghinf.htm (Infantry officers killed 1878–1880, with photographs)

www.garenewing.co.uk/angloafghanwar/waroffice/regiments.php (Regiments involved in the Anglo-Afghan wars 1878–1880)

members.tripod.com/%7EGlosters/guides.htm (List of those killed at the Kabul massacre, with photographs 1879)

AFRICA including BOER & ZULU WARS

en.wikipedia.org/wiki/List_of_conflicts_in_Africa (Links to all African conflicts)

southafricawargraves.org/ (Site of the South African War Graves Project with links, searches and international list of countries with South African war graves)

tinyurl.com/csfufsy (Men who served in the Boer War, from a Leeds plaque)

www.genuki.org.uk/big/eng/DUR/GatesheadWarDead/BoerMemorial.html (Gateshead Boer War casualties) genuki.cs.ncl.ac.uk/DEV/Exeter/WarMemorial.html (Boer War volunteers' memorial list – Exeter)

met.open.ac.uk/genuki/big/eng/bkm/Military/Boer_War/Latimer/ (Name list from Boer War memorial, Latimer, Bucks)

members.tripod.com/%7EGlosters/south.htm (British officers killed in South Africa 1878–1879, with photographs)

www.redcoat.info/sasdlx1.htm (Lists of soldiers killed 1877–1879, from many regiments including Natal mounted police)

members.tripod.com/%7EGlosters/Rhodesia96.htm (British officers killed in Rhodesia 1896)

members.tripod.com/%7EGlosters/africa5.htm (Officers and Royal Marines killed in Africa 1852–1908)

members.tripod.com/%7EGlosters/somali.htm (Officers killed in Somaliland 1901–1904)

ALL GENERAL WARTIME RESOURCES

tinyurl.com/cxl2l9w (Research prisoner of war records at The National Archives – all conflicts)

www.forces-war-records.co.uk/ (Comprehensive wartime records with search facility)

www.veterans-uk.info/ (Veterans Agency website, with links to pensions, welfare services, medals, etc)

www.wartimememories.co.uk/information.html (Wartime Memories Project website)

www.armedforces.co.uk/linksserviceorg.htm (A useful website giving links to lots of service organisations, associations and post-conflict support facilities)

www.britishbattles.com/ (Excellent resource for battles fought by Britain and its Empire forces from the 18th century to the end of the 19th century, illustrated and mapped)

www.historyofwar.org/index.html (Online military encyclopaedia of all war subjects)

www.mick-gray.co.uk/military_sites.htm (Links to military sites of all kinds)

www.genuki.org.uk/big/MilitaryRecords.html (Online leaflets, links and resources)

www.military-genealogy.com/ (Military genealogy specialist website)

www.newarkirregulars.org.uk/links/mhresearch.html (Amazingly comprehensive military history site covering the period from ancient times to the 20th century)

www.iwm.org.uk/ (All about the Imperial War Museum, including family history records)

www.rootsweb.com/~rwguide/lesson13.htm (Hints, tips, international links and addresses, plus a history of military life in Britain)

www.genuki.org.uk/big/MilitaryRecords.html (Genuki's links to military resources) www.old-liverpool.co.uk/Army71.html (Liverpool military families and individuals away from home 1871)

www.wargunner.co.uk/index.htm (War related historical data, links and resources)

www.nationalarchives.gov.uk/catalogue/RdLeaflet.asp?sLeafletID=37 (National Archives resources)

www.historyofwar.org/battleframe.html (Timeline of battles throughout history)

www.angelfire.com/mp/memorials/memindz1.htm (Website collecting British military memorial lists for all wars and campaigns throughout the world)

members.tripod.com/%7EGlosters/guards1.htm (Guards Officers memorial inscriptions – Wellington Barracks – early conflicts 1665–1881)

ANGOLA

balagan.info/timeline-of-the-portuguese-scramble-for-africa (Timeline Portuguese Angola 1884–1917, with maps)

tinyurl.com/br4ucpk (Names and photos of British mercenary soldiers in Angola)

ARMY DOCKYARD VOLUNTEERS

www.genuki.org.uk/big/DockVols.html (List of British Army Dockyard volunteers 1851)

ARMY RECORDS

www.armymuseums.org.uk/ (Records at the Ogilvy Trust)

www.arbeia.demon.co.uk/museums/location/uk/ukmilmus.htm (List of regimental museums)

www.national-army-museum.ac.uk/research/ (National Army Museum for researching military career of relative and related subjects)

www.genuki.org.uk/big/BritMilRecs.html (Page explaining what records are available when searching for a military ancestor)

www.parishchest.com/Military_Matters__LDD1786 (British Army Lists available for purchase on CD)

http://homepage.ntlworld.com/jeffery.knaggs/l1100a.html (Soldiers and others at Borden Camp Military Barracks, Headley, Alton, Hampshire, in 1901 census)

http://homepage.ntlworld.com/jeffery.knaggs/l0612c.html (Soldiers in Isolation Hospital, Mandora Barracks (Aldershot), Surrey)

http://homepage.ntlworld.com/jeffery.knaggs/l0851b.html (List of those in the Beach Rocks Convalescent Home, Sandgate, Kent, at the 1901 census)

www.roll-of-honour.org.uk/ (Roll of honour database covering all classes of people who

died in wartime situations)
www.wirksworth.org.uk/A18-DESR.htm (Detailed list of army deserters 1828–1840 from Derbyshire sources)
www.scan.org.uk/researchrtools/military.htm (Miscellaneous military records and transcriptions online)
www.redcoat.info/memindex3.htm (Records of officers killed in multiple campaigns)

ASIA (GENERAL)

www.movinghere.org.uk/galleries/roots/asian/servicerecords/servicerecords.htm (Information on finding records of servicemen recruited in Asia)

AUSTRALIAN & NEW ZEALAND FORCES

australia.gov.au/topics/defence-and-international/military-history (Australian Government military resources)
www.genealogylinks.net/australia/all-australia/military.htm (Australian forces records links)
search.ancestry.co.uk/search/db.aspx?dbid=1832 (New Zealand Army WWII Nominal Rolls, 1939–1948)
www.exploregenealogy.co.uk/AustraliaMilitaryRecords.html (Australian military records)
members.iinet.net.au/~perthdps/military/links.htm#General (Military links from an Australian perspective)

BORNEO

www.cofepow.org.uk/remembrance/cemeteries/html/borneo.htm (POWs & war graves In Borneo)
www.nmbva.co.uk/army%20Borneo.htm (Army involvement in Borneo)
www.britains-smallwars.com/Borneo/ (Index to Borneo/Malaysia conflicts)
www.ww2australia.gov.au/lastbattles/landings.html (Australian troops in Borneo)
www.seadart.net/tiger/Borneo62.htm (HMS *Tiger* in Borneo 1962)

BURMA

www.cofepow.org.uk/remembrance/cemeteries/html/burma.htm (Burma POW war graves)

members.tripod.com/%7EGlosters/burmamem1.htm (Officers killed in the Burma conflicts 1824– 1930)

members.tripod.com/%7EGlosters/IP1.htm (India and Burma British Police killed 1888–1942)

CANADIAN FORCES

globalgenealogy.com/countries/canada/military/resources/index.htm (List of books for Canadian military research)

www.rootsweb.com/~canmil/index.html (Military history in Canada)

en.wikipedia.org/wiki/Military_history_of_Canada (Overview of Canadian military history)

www.collectionscanada.gc.ca/military-peace/index-e.html (Military collection of Canadian archives)

CHINA

www.history.co.uk/explore-history/ww2/sino-japanese-war.html (China/Japanese conflict, with videos)

en.wikipedia.org/wiki/Opium_Wars (Background to the British involvement in the Chinese Opium Wars 1839–1860)

members.tripod.com/%7EGlosters/china60.htm (British Officers who died in China 1842–1901)

CIVIL WAR IN AMERICA

www.acws.co.uk/ (American Civil War Society pages)

www.h2g2.com/approved_entry/A912386 (About Britain's involvement in the American Civil War)

www.militaryindexes.com/civilwar/ (U.S. Civil War links and resources)

CIVIL WAR IN ENGLAND

www.nationalarchives.gov.uk/education/civilwar/g5/key/ (The National Archives guide to the Civil War)

www.british-history.ac.uk/search.asp?query1=civil+war (Official documents referring to the Civil War period)

www.historyonthenet.com/Civil_War/civilwarmain.htm (English Civil War information)

www.british-history.ac.uk/search.asp?query1=interregnum (Official records of the Interregnum and Civil War period)

www.british-history.ac.uk/search.asp?query1=civil+war (Specific records dealing with the Civil War in England)

www.british-history.ac.uk/search.asp?query1=Royalist+composition+papers (Access to various Royalist Composition records)

CIVILIAN WAR DEAD

www.historylearningsite.co.uk/civilian_casualties_of_world_war.htm (Chart of WWII civilian deaths by country)

www.liverpoolmonuments.co.uk/warmemorials/bootle.htm (Bootle's WWII civilian war dead)

www.liverpoolmonuments.co.uk/warmemorials/wardead1940.htm (Liverpool 1940 casualties)

www.genuki.org.uk/big/eng/Indexes/NE_WarDead/ (List of WWII civilians killed by enemy action in Northumberland, Durham and Yorkshire)

www.roll-of-honour.com/Kent/AshfordCivilian.html (Ashford, Kent's civilians killed during WWII)

www.chrishobbs.com/sheffield/pitsmoorwardead.htm (Sheffield roll of honour)

CONSCIENTIOUS OBJECTORS TO MILITARY SERVICE

www.nationalarchives.gov.uk/catalogue/RdLeaflet.asp?sLeafletID=25 (National Archives' guide to tracing conscientious objectors and those exempt from service)

www.historylearningsite.co.uk/conscientious_objectors.htm (WWI Conscientious Objectors)

www.nationalarchives.gov.uk/pathways/firstworldwar/spotlights/antiwar.htm (All about the Anti-War Movement)

CRIMEAN WAR

cwrs.russianwar.co.uk (Crimean War Society Research Society)
www.nationalarchives.gov.uk/records/looking-for-subject/crimeanwar.htm (National Archives page)
www.british-genealogy.com/forums/forumdisplay.php?f=311 (Crimean War forum)
www.roll-of-honour.com/Databases/Crimea30thFootCasualties/index.html (Search for Crimean casualties of the 30th foot)

EGYPT 1882-1885 & SUDAN 1896-1897

search.ancestry.co.uk/search/db.aspx?dbid=1686 (Trace medal awards from these conflicts here)
www.naval-military-press.com/egypt-1882-89/ (A source of books for researchers)
members.tripod.com/%7EGlosters/egyptz.htm (List of Officers killed, with some photographs)
www.redcoat.info/egyptroll82.htm (Soldiers killed in Egypt 1882–1885)

EVACUEES

clutch.open.ac.uk/schools/standrews00/evac_nthbucks.htm (Information about evacuation in Buckinghamshire)
www.war-experience.org/education/evacuation/evacuation-intro.asp (Background to the evacuee plans, plus link to personal stories)
www.bbc.co.uk/schoolradio/subjects/history/ww2clips/eyewitness/evacuees/ (Evacuees – interviews and videos)

FALKLANDS WAR 1982

britains-smallwars.com/Falklands/roh.html (Falklands War page of remembrance)
www.raf.mod.uk/history/ArmyFalklandIslandsRollofHonour.cfm (Roll of honour of all servicemen who fought this war)
http://members.tripod.com/%7EGlosters/falkland.htm (Army Officers killed in 1982 – includes those from other services also)
www.britains-smallwars.com/Falklands/roh.html (Falklands War page of remembrance)

INDIAN CONFLICTS

search.ancestry.co.uk/search/category.aspx?cat=39 (Search Ancestry's military records)

members.tripod.com/%7EGlosters/memindex3.htm (List of those who died during the Indian Mutiny, plus lots of other campaigns)

members.tripod.com/%7EGlosters/punniar.htm (Officers killed at Punniar and Maharajpore, India 1843)

members.tripod.com/%7EGlosters/Mudki.htm (Officers who died at Battle of Mudki, 1845)

members.tripod.com/%7EGlosters/Feroz.htm (Officers who died at Battle of Ferozsha, 1845)

members.tripod.com/%7EGlosters/Aliwal.htm (Officers who died in Battles of Badhowal, Aliwal and Sobraon, 1846)

www.redcoat.info/sutsl1.htm (Sutlej Campaign casualties listed alphabetically)

members.tripod.com/%7EGlosters/murder48.htm (British representatives murdered at Punjab, sparking the Punjab campaign)

members.tripod.com/%7EGlosters/Multan.htm (Officers who died at the siege of Multan, 1848–1849)

members.tripod.com/%7EGlosters/Chili.htm (British Officers 1849 who died at Battle of Chillianwala and Heights of Dullah, plus native officers)

members.tripod.com/%7EGlosters/Gujerat.htm (Officers who died at Battle of Gujarat, 1849)

members.tripod.com/%7EGlosters/Ramnag.htm (Officers who died at Ramnagur, 1848)

http://members.tripod.com/%7EGlosters/Exped.htm (Indians who died in the various Indian Expeditions, 1850–1888, including Persia [Iran] and Bhutan)

members.tripod.com/%7EGlosters/india1908.htm (Officers killed in India 1908–1947)

IRAQ

tinyurl.com/cqx3tgj (Iraq conflict images – click image for web link)

www.redcoat.info/iraq2003.htm (List of Officers killed in Afghanistan and Iraq conflicts 2003–2009)

www.guardian.co.uk/world/2007/feb/05/iraq.military1 (List of soldiers killed in Iraq)

IRELAND

www.bbc.co.uk/history/recent/troubles/the_troubles_article_01.shtml (Irish troubles 1963–1985 from the BBC)

members.tripod.com/%7EGlosters/Ireland16.htm (British Officers and RUC officers killed in Irish Rebellion 1916)

members.tripod.com/%7EGlosters/ulster6999.htm (Officers killed in Northern Ireland 1969–1999)

homepage.eircom.net/~tipperaryfame/ireland.htm (Irish conflicts website)

en.wikipedia.org/wiki/Irish_Volunteers (Information about the Irish Volunteers military organisation)

JACOBITE & WILLIAMITE CONFLICTS

en.wikipedia.org/wiki/Williamite_war_in_Ireland (Jacobite war in Ireland)

www.british-history.ac.uk/search.asp?query1=jacobites (Online resources and document transcriptions)

www.jacobite.ca/essays/index.htm (Jacobite essays & resources)

www.nationalarchives.gov.uk/catalogue/RdLeaflet.asp?sLeafletID=87 (National Archives fact sheet –records held regarding Jacobite Risings of 1715 & 1745)

www.northumbrianjacobites.org.uk/ (The Northumbrian Jacobite Society home page)

www.nas.gov.uk/guides/military.asp (Guide to Jacobite and other military records in Scottish National Archives)

www.rls.org.uk/database/record.php?usi=000-000-001-458-L (Illustrated study pack of Jacobite Rebellion 1745 and Culloden)

www.foda.org.uk/oaths/intro/introduction4.htm (Names of Jacobite supporters in Devon)

JAPAN

www.history.co.uk/explore-history/ww2/sino-japanese-war.html (China/Japanese conflict with videos)

www.fsmitha.com/h2/ch23ja.html (About the war against Japan 1942–45)

www.history.army.mil/books/amh/amh-23.htm (History of the war against Japan)

JAVA REGION

www.roll-of-honour.org.uk/atrocities/600%5FGunners%5FParty/index.htm (Database of British prisoners and survivors of the 600 Gunners Party)

members.tripod.com/%7EGlosters/java.htm (Officers killed at Java, Isle of France, Mauritius 1810–1813)

KOREA

www.archives.gov/research/military/korean-war/index.html (Links to Korean War websites, including casualties)
www.militaryindexes.com/koreanwar/index.html (Online Korean War resources)
members.tripod.com/%7EGlosters/koreaomem1.htm (British officers killed 1950–1953)

KOSOVO

en.wikipedia.org/wiki/Kosovo_War (All about the Kosovo conflict with links)
www.iwm.org.uk/search/global?query=kosovo&.x=0&.y=0 (Imperial War Museum pages)

MALAYA 1948–1962

www.britains-smallwars.com/malaya/reg.html (British and Commonwealth Units that participated in the Malayan Emergency)
members.tripod.com/%7EGlosters/malaya.htm (List of officers killed)

MALAYSIA / MALLACA / BRUNEI & SARAWAK

members.tripod.com/%7EGlosters/malacca31.htm (Short list of officers killed in Malacca)
members.tripod.com/%7EGlosters/perak.htm (Officers/men at Perak, 1876–77)
www.britains-smallwars.com/Borneo (Index to Malaysia Peninsula conflicts)

MALTA

durhamlightinfantry.webs.com/maltagc.htm (Durham Light Infantry in Malta)
www.maltafamilyhistory.com/ (British Forces family history connections in Malta)
www.visitmalta.com/en/british-period (Malta – the British period, including link to a list of ex-servicemen)

MAORI WARS / NEW ZEALAND WARS

tinyurl.com/ckht3g8 (Involvement of the 70th (Surrey) Regiment)

www.redcoat.info/nzwar.htm (Officers who died during the conflicts 1844–1864)

www.redcoat.info/nzwar1.htm (Soldiers and navy personnel 1845–1864)

MEDALS

search.ancestry.co.uk/search/db.aspx?dbid=1686 (UK, Military Campaign Medal and Award Rolls, 1793–1949)

tinyurl.com/co8xate (National Archives' guide to medal records – search WWI medal rolls online)

www.worldmedals.co.uk/Rib/Britrib/britribb.htm (Illustrated British medals list – commercial site)

www.mod.uk/DefenceInternet/ContactUs/MedalsEnquiries.htm (Enquiry form for Army, Navy or Air Force medals)

www.victoriacrosssociety.com/links.htm (Victoria Cross Society website, with links for researchers)

www.marionhebblethwaite.co.uk/gcindex.htm (Database of holders of the George Cross)

www.medals.org.uk/ (Searchable Medals of the World website)

www.burmastar.org.uk/military_history1.htm (Burma Star military history links)

www.stephen-stratford.co.uk/wwii_medals.htm (All about WWII medals – illustrated)

www.royalhumanesociety.org.uk/html/research_request.html (Researching the Archives of the Royal Humane Society & medal awards)

MERCENARIES (all conflicts)

tinyurl.com/bovofox (Google's list of pages about British mercenaries in all conflicts)

www.ww2talk.com/forum/postwar/23979-angola-1976-trial-british-mercenaries.html (British mercenaries in Angola WWII)

NAPOLEONIC WARS

www.napoleonguide.com/battle_trafalgar.htm (Outline of battle of Trafalgar, with Napoleonic links)

www.genuki.org.uk/big/eng/Trafalgar/ (Names of ships, officers and men who fought at Trafalgar on 21st October 1805)

www.nationalarchives.gov.uk/trafalgarancestors/ (Search for men who fought at the battle of Trafalgar)

www.napoleon-series.org/military/organization/c_spanish.html (Spanish recruits in the British Army 1812–1813)

members.tripod.com/%7EGlosters/allwat.htm (Peninsular/Waterloo veterans 1800s)

members.tripod.com/%7EGlosters/QB1.htm (Quatre-Bras officers and regiments 1815)

www.old-liverpool.co.uk/Waterloo.html (Lancashire men in Battle of Waterloo)

www.genuki.org.uk/big/Helena.html (List of those on the Island of St Helena during Napoleon's detention there 1815–1821)

PENSION & SERVICE RECORDS (ALL SERVICES)

www.archives.gov/research/order/order-vets-records.html (Access to Military Service and Pensions information)

www.nationalarchives.gov.uk/pathways/firstworldwar/service_records/ sr_soldiers.htm (Guide and links for all services pensions)

www.movinghere.org.uk/galleries/roots/jewish/service/service.htm (Jewish service records)

www.24hourmuseum.org.uk/nwh_gfx_en/ART44213.html (Accessing WWII pension records online)

www.nationalarchives.gov.uk/records/looking-for-person/royalnavyrating 1853-1923.htm (How to obtain Navy service records)

PORTUGAL COLONIAL CONFLICTS

en.wikipedia.org/wiki/Portuguese_Colonial_War (Portuguese Colonial War)

www.portugaldailyview.com/whats-new/colonial-war-the-wounds-of-the- portuguese-vietnam-in-africa (Personal experiences and photos regarding the wounds of the Portuguese Vietnam in Africa)

PRISONERS OF WAR & INTERNEES

www.historylearningsite.co.uk/british_internees.htm (Resources regarding interned British civilians living in Germany during WWII)

www.isle-of-man.com/manxnotebook/famhist/genealgy/intern.htm (Internment camps in the Isle of Man)

www.nationalarchives.gov.uk/documentsonline/pow.asp (National Archives' resources)

www.petrowilliamus.co.uk/murals/murals.htm (Site dedicated to the murals painted by POWs in Changi camp)

www.historylearningsite.co.uk/changi_pow_camp.htm (Another Changi POW site)

home.comcast.net/~winjerd/POWCamp1.htm (An insight into life and death at a POW camp in wartime Japan)

www.historylearningsite.co.uk/colditz.htm (Colditz POW camp resource page)

www.powtaiwan.org/ (Taiwan POWs database with search facility)

www.movinghere.org.uk/galleries/roots/asian/pullingittogether/pows.htm (Asiatic Merchant seamen POWs information)

www.pcf.city.hiroshima.jp/index_e2.html (Hiroshima Memorial Museum)

RED CROSS/RED CRESCENT WORKERS

www.historylearningsite.co.uk/red_cross_and_world_war_two.htm (Details of the work of the Red Cross in WWII)

www.redcross.org.uk/About-us/Who-we-are/Museum-and-archives (British Red Cross Museum and Archives, with links to WWI and WWII workers)

www.redcross.int/en/history/archive.asp (Access to International Red Cross/Red Crescent archives)

www.redcross.org.uk/standard.asp?id=3008&cachefixer (Missing people in WWI and WWII via Red Cross)

REGIMENTAL INFORMATION

en.wikipedia.org/wiki/Regimental_museum (Regimental museums list)

www.indiaman.com/ (British regiments in Asia)

www.victoriacross.org.uk/ccregmus.htm (List of Regimental Museums)

battlefields1418.50megs.com/british_regiments.htm (British regiments in WWI)

www.jaunay.com/garrisons.html (British regiments in Australia 1788–1870)

users.netconnect.com.au/~ianmac/britain.html (British forces in Victoria, Australia)

freepages.history.rootsweb.com/~garter1/tobegin.htm (Australia's British 'Red Coat Regiments' with names)

www.roll-of-honour.com/Regiments/ (Regimental rolls of honour links and searches)
www.black-history.org.uk/blacksoldiers.asp (Information regarding black soldiers serving in British regiments in the 19th century)
www.electricscotland.com/history/scotreg/ (Scottish regimental information)
custermen.com/ItalyWW2/ArmyOrg/BritishOrg.htm (Information regarding British regiments in Italy WWII)
battlefieldsww2.50megs.com/normandy_unit_profiles.htm (British regiments in Normandy WWII)

ROYAL AIR FORCE & FLEET AIR ARM

www.raf.mod.uk/search/index.cfm (RAF rolls of honour)
www.iwm.org.uk/search/global?query=raf+records&x=0&y=0 (Information on tracing RAF service records)
www.nationalarchives.gov.uk/records/research-guides/raf-service-1939-1945.htm (WWII RAF service records)
www.raf.mod.uk/history/ (General history of the RAF)
www.raf.mod.uk/links/contacts.cfm (Help with tracing Air Force records)
www.fleetairarmarchive.net/ (The Fleet Air Arm archives)

ROYAL NAVY & MARINES

www.rtna.ac.th/article/Navy%20Slang%20Dictionary%20-%20pdf%20Version.pdf (A guide to naval slang)
www.nationalarchives.gov.uk/documentsonline/royal-navy-service.asp (Details of how to search and download details of over 500,000 Royal Navy seamen 1873–1923)
homepage.ntlworld.com/jeffery.knaggs/I0732c.html (List of those at Royal Marine Barracks, Chatham, Kent, at 1901 census)
homepage.ntlworld.com/jeffery.knaggs/I2377a.html (List of those on HMS *Formidable* – training ship, off Portishead, Bristol Channel, at 1901 census)
www.pbenyon.plus.com/NZ_Xross_Line/P15.html (Ship's company of HMS *New Zealand*,1919)
www.angelfire.com/de/BobSanders/Site.html (Navy and maritime research links and resources)
www.pbenyon.plus.com/Naval.html (Lots of miscellaneous Naval and Maritime resources)
www.genuki.org.uk/big/FlgOff1.html (Naval and marine officers listed in the Naval and Military Almanac 1840 A-H)

www.genuki.org.uk/big/FlgOff2.html (Naval and marine officers listed in the Naval and Military Almanac 1840 I-Y)

homepage.ntlworld.com/jeffery.knaggs/RNShips.html (1901 index of Royal Navy ships and their positions, captains, etc)

www.fleetairarmarchive.net/Ships/Index.html (WWII aircraft carrier and other Naval shipping links)

www.genuki.org.uk/big/eng/Trafalgar/ (Names of ships, officers and men who fought at Trafalgar on 21st October 1805)

www.nationalarchives.gov.uk/documentsonline/royal-navy-service.asp (How to consult details of over 600,000 Royal Navy seamen 1873–1923)

SCOTTISH MILITARY RESEARCH

www.nas.gov.uk/guides/military.asp (National Archives of Scotland military records)

www.scotlandspeople.gov.uk/content/help/index.aspx?965 (Scottish Military research tips and links)

http://www.scottishmilitaryresearch.org.uk/ (Scottish Military History website)

SEVEN YEARS WAR (1756–1763)

tinyurl.com/ckryrc6 (Google's links to the Seven Years War)

www.historyofwar.org/articles/wars_sevenyears.html (A site dedicated to the Seven Years War)

SPANISH CIVIL WAR

discovery.nationalarchives.gov.uk/SearchUI/browse/C11541641 (UK volunteers' records in National Archives)

www.guardian.co.uk/commentisfree/2011/jun/28/mi5-spanish-civil-war-britain (About MI5 records of UK volunteers in Spain)

TERRITORIALS, MILITIA, FENCIBLES & YEOMANRY

www.nationalarchives.gov.uk/records/research-guides/army-auxiliary-1769-1945.htm (NA guide to Auxiliary forces records 1769–1945)

en.wikipedia.org/wiki/Territorial_Army_(United_Kingdom) (WWI Territorial Forces, with links to regiments and divisions)

www.genuki.org.uk/search/ (Genuki search engine – Type in the word 'militia' to access over 1000 entries on the subject)

http://en.wikipedia.org/wiki/List_of_British_fencible_regiments (Lists of British Fencible regiments)

www.genuki.org.uk/big/eng/YKS/Misc/Military/Militia1.html (List of officers in North Yorkshire Militia 1758–1907)

genuki.cs.ncl.ac.uk/DEV/DevonIndexes/NorthDevonYeomanry.html (Members of the North Devon Yeomanry 1794–1924)

US FORCES & WARS

www.history.army.mil/ (US Army Centre of Military History)

www.militaryindexes.com/civilwar/ (US Civil War links and resources)

genrootsblog.blogspot.com/2006/07/civil-war-pension-service-records-tips.html (Aid to finding US Civil War pension and service records)

www.carolyar.com/1812.htm (Records of 1812 war between Britain and America)

www.cyndislist.com/military.htm (Lots of links to US military resources)

VIETNAM WAR

tinyurl.com/oswrxob (Britain's involvement in Vietnam war, with video)

WAR BRIDES

www.geocities.com/us_warbrides/ (Site dedicated to U.S. war brides, with lots of interesting genealogy add-ons)

www.passengerlists.co.uk/search.htm (Search war brides on passenger ships)

www.canadianwarbrides.com/passenger-lists.asp (War brides bound for Canada)

WAR GRAVES & MEMORIALS

www.cwgc.org/ (Commonwealth War Graves Commission site – free search for graves and memorials online, also civilian roll of honour)

www.ukniwm.org.uk/ (Search the National Inventory of War Graves)

www.wartimememories.co.uk/information.html (International war graves links)

www.warmemorials.org (Website of War Memorials Trust)

www.essex.police.uk/system_pages/search_site.aspx?terms=memoria l (Essex Police Memorial Trust website)

www.roll-of-honour.com/ (War memorials throughout the country plus supplementary war information)

www.genuki.org.uk/big/eng/Indexes/NE_WarDead/Abbreviations.html (Abbreviations found on rolls of honour and war memorials)
www.angelfire.com/mp/memorials/memindz1.htm (Website collecting British military memorial lists for all wars and campaigns throughout the world)
members.tripod.com/%7EGlosters/guards1.htm (Guards Officers memorial inscriptions – Wellington Barracks, early conflicts1665–1881)
www.genuki.org.uk/big/eng/Indexes/NE_WarDead/ (List of WWII civilians killed by enemy action in Northumberland, Durham and Yorkshire)

WAR OF 1812

tinyurl.com/brwucyo (Google's links to the war of 1812)
www.warof1812.ca/1812link.htm (Links and information regarding British involvement)
www.carolyar.com/1812.htm (Website dedicated to the 1812 war between Britain and America)

WOMEN AT WAR

www.nationalarchives.gov.uk/documentsonline/waac.asp (Women's Army Auxiliary Corps records at The National Archives)
www.users.zetnet.co.uk/dms/past/ww1/women.html (Photographs of women in the services WWI)
www.scarletfinders.co.uk/ (Military nursing website)
www.wartimememoriesproject.com/ww2/homefront/womenslandarmy.php (Information, memories and photographs about the Women's Land Army)
www.spartacus.schoolnet.co.uk/2WWlandarmy.htm (General website about Women's Land Army)
www.cyber-heritage.co.uk/ww2women/ (Portrayals of women in WWII advertising)

WORLD WAR I

www.nationalarchives.gov.uk/documentsonline/medals.asp (WWI medal index cards)
www.iwm.org.uk/ (Imperial War Museum site)
www.cwgc.org/somme/ (Battle of the Somme: day-by-day account, with detailed maps and photograph gallery)
www.ewhurstfallen.co.uk/Roll%20of%20Honour.htm (A list of those who died in WWI from Ewhurst and Ellen's Green, Surrey)
www.barton-under-needwood.org.uk/rolhon.html (WWI and WWII war Roll of Honour from Barton-under-Needwood, Staffs.)

www.genuki.org.uk/search/ (Type the words 'roll of honour' into this search engine to find nearly a thousand lists of war dead and similar web pages throughout Britain and Ireland)
www.hellotommy.co.uk/Great_War_Links/great_war_links.html (A good selection of WWI links)
www.hertfordshire-genealogy.co.uk/data/occupations/military-ww1.htm (Various links regarding WWI in Hertfordshire)
www.worldwar1.com/tsearch.htm (Search facility for WWI information)
net.lib.byu.edu/~rdh7/wwi/ (WWI document archive)
www.hellfirecorner.co.uk (Hellfire Corner – stories and anecdotes from WWI)

WORLD WAR II

www.familyrelatives.com/navigate/navigate_detail.php?id=16 (Family Relatives WWII page)
www.iwm.org.uk/ (Imperial War Museum site)
www.secondworldwar.co.uk/links.html (Page with some unusual WWII links)
www.britain-at-war.org.uk/html/links.htm (Links to records and resources)
www.ers.cqm.co.uk/rservice/wwlk.htm (Scottish WWII links)
www.wartimememories.co.uk/links.html (Wartime Memories Project page with lots of useful links)
www.primaryresources.co.uk/history/history1.htm (Primary resources website with some unusual links)
www.ibiblio.org/pha/ (List of links to World War II resources)
www.war-experience.org/index.html (Second World War Experience Centre resources page)
www.ww2poster.co.uk/ (Site concentrating on World War II posters)
www.atomicbombmuseum.org (The Atom Bomb Museum website)
www.roll-of-honour.com/Regiments/ (Rolls of honour by regiment with search facilities)
www.bbc.co.uk/history/worldwars/wwtwo/ (BBC site about WWII, with links)
www.codesandciphers.org.uk/lorenz/fish.htm (Details about the use of codes in WWII and those involved)
www.cyber-heritage.co.uk/cutaway/ (Site dedicated to WWII images)
www.worldwar-2.net/ (WWII timeline)

Royal Artillery Clerks' Training Group in the Second World War.
© *2014 Colin Waters Collection*

WILLS, ADMINISTRATION, PROBATE & DEATH DUTIES

Wills, administration and probate records are invaluable to family history research because they give us details of names, relationships, locations of property and land. In addition they provide insights into the lifestyle of our ancestors. Strictly, a will contains the actual instructions given by a person as to what should be done about his or her affairs after death, whilst a testament referred to the distribution of his or her property. Inventories of the deceased person's possessions often accompany old wills and testaments. The distinction between these documents has been blurred in modern times and many aspects are combined in a modern will. Probate is the legal process of settling the estate of a deceased person by officially resolving all claims and sanctioning the distribution of the property. All wills and administrations (often referred to as 'admons' and issued if there was no will) proven in England and Wales after 1858 are held in the Principal Registry of the Family Division in Holborn. Holdings are indexed alphabetically by surname and year and the entries contain valuable name, address and occupational details. Before 1858 wills were proved in a multitude of local Church courts. Death Duty registers record wills and bequests for estates liable to death duties.

www.nationalwillsindex.com/ (National Wills Index)
tinyurl.com/d45aam9 (Thousands of links to British and Irish will resources)
www.genuki.org.uk/big/eng/Probate.html (County by county guide to English probate record sources)
nationalarchives.gov.uk/documentsonline/wills.asp (Search wills proved at the Prerogative Court of Canterbury 1384–1858 online)
www.york.ac.uk/library/borthwick/research-support/research-guides/ (A simple guide to finding probate records)
www.ukdocuments.com/ (Commercial site offering to search official probate indexes from 11th January 1858 onwards)
www.hmcourts-service.gov.uk/cms/1226.htm (Government site with a guide to obtaining copies of probate records)
www.medievalgenealogy.org.uk/sources/probate.shtml (Site with links to medieval probate records and resources throughout Britain)
www.wills4all.netfirms.com/names_in_wills.htm (Growing list of names found in wills throughout Britain)
west-penwith.org.uk/probate/index.htm (West Penwith probate records online)
www.wirksworth.org.uk/B60-WBRA.htm (Some Derbyshire probates 1535–1800)
webs.lanset.com/azazella/probate_supp.html (Cornish probate records)
www.archives.norfolk.gov.uk/Archive-Collections/index.htm (Guide to Norfolk probate record holdings)

www.wirksworth.org.uk/WILLS.htm (Derbyshire wills)

www.wirksworth.org.uk/WAdX1.htm#A (Derbyshire administrations list)

www.nationalarchives.gov.uk/documentsonline/wills.asp (Search wills at The National Archives)

www.thegenealogist.co.uk/ (Subscription site – Search for and view actual wills)

tinyurl.com/cmabvvk (Search death duty registers 1796–1903 online at The National Archives)

www.findmypast.co.uk/DeathDutyStartSearchServlet (Search death duty registers)

To find more books on Family History and Genealogy please visit our website:
www.countrysidebooks.co.uk

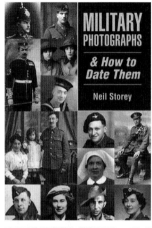

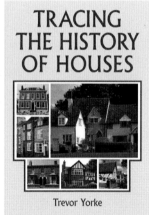

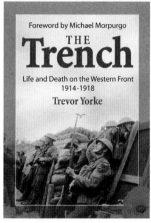

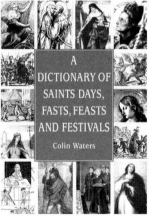

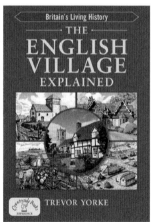

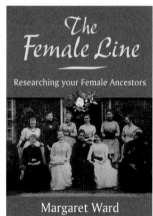

Like us on Facebook – **Countryside Books**